ROCK ON!

The Rock 'n' Roll Greats

Colin King

Acknowledgments:

Courtesy of Redferns Music Picture Library:

p.7, 13, 15, 19, 23, 25, 27, 29, 35, 38, 39, 45, 49, 50, 53, 55, 71, 80, 82, 83, 84, 86, 91 and 93 (Michael Ochs Archive); p.17, 37, 64-65, 69, 73, 102 and 109 (David Redfern); p.21, 30, 47, 61, 87, 111 and 115 (Glen A. Baker); p. 76-77 and 101 (Chuck Boyd); p.11 (Deltahaze Corporation); p.32-33 (Leon Morris); p.58 (David Farrell); p.66 (Brown Packaging Books Ltd); p.62 (Max Scheler); p.43 (New Eyes); p41 (Andrew Putler); p.74 (Cyrus Andrews); p. 92 (John Rogers); p. 95 (Gunter Zint); p.79 and 97 (Elliot Landy); p.98 (Herbe Greene); p.105 (Harry Goodwin); p.112 (RB); p.106-107 (John Marshall); p.117 (Peter Still); p. 118 (Howard Barlow); p. 121 (Richard E. Aaron); p. 122 (Ebet Roberts); p123 (Erica Echenberg)

Published in 2002 by Caxton Editions
20 Bloomsbury Street
London WC1B 3JH
a member of the Caxton Publishing Group

© 2002 Caxton Publishing Group

Designed and produced for Caxton Editions
by Open Door Limited
Langham, Rutland
Editing: Mary Morton
Setting: Jane Booth
Colour Separation: GA Graphics, Stamford, UK

Title: 'Rock On' The Rock 'n' Roll Greats
ISBN: 1 84067 473 3

ROCK ON!

The Rock 'n' Roll Greats

Colin King

CAXTON EDITIONS

CONTENTS

CONTENTS

INTRODUCTION

This book will reveal the history of rock 'n' roll music, from its early origins in the area of Africa which is now Nigeria through to the clinical ambience of today's computerised recording. In tracing the history of rock 'n' roll music we will show how the particular kind of music of which the term 'rock 'n' roll' was first used in the 1950s metamorphosed through the 60s into the music that has been classified as 'rock' ever since.

It is difficult to say exactly when rock 'n' roll started as the term had been in use amongst African Americans to describe lovemaking long before it came to signify a music style. Alan Freed, the New York disc jockey, was supposed to have coined the phrase in 1951 and rose to fame through his radio show Moondog's Rock 'n' Roll Party but, as a musical genre, rock 'n' roll did not make an impact on the general public until 1953 when 'Crazy Man Crazy' by Bill Haley and his Comets became the first rock 'n' roll song to make the best-selling list on *Billboard*'s national chart.

Rock 'n' roll is a mishmash of musical styles. The African Americans supplied the beat, the European Americans supplied the melodies through their folk songs and by the 1960s the British influence became an integral part of its development. What made it different from the generally accepted popular music was the rise of youth culture. In its early days its audience was in many ways a secret one: teenagers lying awake under their bedclothes, listening to their transistor radios through the night. For the medium that spread rock 'n' roll was the radio above all, especially the transistor which was then, in the 1950s, a new invention.

In the early part of the 1960s America, the melting pot of rock 'n' roll, was invaded by British bands, particularly the Beatles, and during the latter part of the 1960s the psychedelic West Coast bands came to the fore. The 1970s saw the rise of 'Glam Rock' and in the latter part of the decade 'Punk Rock' and with the invention of the synthesiser the 1980s began the era of 'Electronic Pop Rock' which continues to this day.

'Nothing more than an exhibition of primitive tom-tom thumping, rock 'n' roll has been played in the jungle for centuries'

SIR MALCOLM SARGENT

Right: the medium that spread rock 'n' roll was the radio transistor.

Above: The undisputed king of rock 'n' roll.

THE EARLY ORIGINS OF ROCK 'N' ROLL

The most influential music in the world, rock 'n' roll, originated from an African drumbeat blended with the folk melodies of Europe and was fused in America. Popular music has absorbed these influences and through the media of records, radio stations, videos and television what was once a distant drumbeat from a small Nigerian village has become the musical voice of the people of the Western world.

Millions of African men, women and children, particularly those of West Africa, were brought to the 'New World' by the slave traders after the Americas were colonised. The slave ships had no room for possessions and slaves had to leave all their worldly belongings behind. The plantation owners believed that the more they could remove of the slaves' former culture, the more easy they would be to control. However, it was impossible to remove the rhythm and the tribal chants and the slaves adapted them as work songs.

These rhythms consisted of the three-drum grouping found in the Yoruba tribes of Western and Central Africa. The Yoruba 'bata' drums consist of three drums, representing a family. The largest bata drum (*iya*) represents the father in terms of its role. The middle drum (*itotele*) is the mother, and the smallest, and therefore the highest-pitched, is the child (*okonkolo*). The father drum leads the family by dictating the changes in rhythm and leads the 'conversation'. The mother drum plays a fixed pattern until the father instructs otherwise. Lastly the child drum plays a repetitive and fixed pattern. The drums create rhyth-

mic tension within the group dynamic, with the parent drums pulling on the beat, so creating a more laid-back feel. Meanwhile the child drum always pushes – that is, plays on top of the beat. These three drums eventually evolved into the modern drum kit of bass, tom and snare.

Some of the slaves who had lived in the Islamic regions of West Africa also brought with them the Arabic rhythms which had been mixed into the African tribal rhythms. These rhythms involved a deep bass drum, syncopated hand-clapping and 'call and response' vocal interplay. This music was particularly used for an Islamic holy circle dance where the pilgrims circumambulated Islam's most sacred shrine in Mecca, always in an anticlockwise direction. This act of worship was called the *saut*, pronounced shout, and this became the inspiration for the slave shout songs and ring dances. The Joujouka drummers of Morocco who inspired Brian Jones of the Rolling Stones continue this tradition to the present day.

The main difference between African and European music is that African music is polyrhythmic (composed of the juxtaposition of many complementary and contradictory rhythms) whilst European music is polyphonic (composed of the juxtaposition of many contradictory and complementary tones). This is not to say that melody and tone or rhythm are excluded from either form. Instead each culture focused and organised its approach to making music around a different central premise.

Traditional African musicians, who focused on rhythm rather than tone, added a variety of shadings around the tones. This caused their notes to sound imprecise to European ears. Also the modal scales employed were different. In standard European music the diatonic scale is used (do, re, mi, fa, sol, la, ti, do) and so, in order to work with the tuning of European instruments, black American musicians created the so-called 'blue notes' (the flattened fifth and seventh notes of the eight-note diatonic scale). With guitars, for example, they ran knife blades or bottle necks along the metal strings of the fretboard to change the pure notes that the instruments were designed to produce. Another technique was to slap and pull at the strings to increase the 'dissonant' effect, rather than the usual strumming.

In the American South there was a long-standing tradition of both slaves and free black musicians entertaining audiences of mixed races. The slave musicians learnt either 'by ear' or through apprenticeship to another folk musician. They utilised and adapted whatever could be made into or already was an instrument. The black musicians approached the European instruments with an African consciousness, so creating a new form of music.

This was called 'Blues' music because of the blue notes used and was a music of celebration, played to accompany revellers at ecstatic, all-night country dances. These dances retained elements of African tribal rhythms and the 'bluesmen' served as jukeboxes. Each piece that was performed would last as long as the dancers wanted it to, sometimes an hour or more. Because of the length of these pieces, the bluesmen improvised new verses and instrumental variations to the background of the tribal drumming rhythms.

This 'Blues' music evolved into the recognisable 12 'bars' sometime around the start of the 20th century. However, because this was before the era of sound recording, it is impossible to state precisely when it started. Recording of this African-American music began during the 1920s. Owing to the short playing time of the 78 rpm record, these long improvisations were shortened to the three minutes that could be put onto a record. Although these three-minute pieces were vastly shortened versions of the original hour-long improvisations, the general public viewed these forced abridgements as the final and fixed version of a particular song, which is something their creators never intended.

As a result of this process, the music was no longer African or European. It was a vital new hybrid, a truly American music. During the following years the general public came to accept this mixture of polyrhythmic and polytonic music, with its note bending, slurring, 'call and response' vocal pattern and shout songs which caused it to be absorbed into the language of mainstream popular music all over the world.

The most famous bluesmen of this time who left recordings of their performances were Charley Patton, Son House and, most importantly, Robert Johnson.

BIOGRAPHY:

Robert Johnson

Robert Johnson was born in Hazlehurst, Mississippi. In his teens he learnt guitar from teachers including Charley Patton and Son House. Legend has it that Johnson sold his soul to the devil at a crossroads in exchange for guitar-playing prowess.

During the Depression years Johnson earned his keep as an entertainer. His travels took him throughout the Mississippi and Arkansas Deltas, where he performed at juke joints, levee camps and country suppers. He also went to the big cities, travelling with fellow bluesman Johnny Shines, and performed in St Louis, Detroit and Chicago. He became the first musician to link the country blues of the Mississippi Delta with the city blues of the post-World War II era.

He only had two recording sessions in his brief career. The first spanned three days in November 1936 and the second two days in June 1937, yielding 29 songs in all, 22 of which appeared on 78 rpm singles from the Vocalion label. The first and most popular was 'Terraplane Blues', followed by other classics such as 'Cross Road Blues', 'Love In Vain' and 'Sweet Home Chicago'.

On 13 August 1938 he was poisoned by the jealous husband of a woman he had been seeing during his residency at the Three Forks juke joint in Greenwood, Mississippi. Three days later he died at the home of a friend. His 'supernatural' prowess changed the direction of American music and is the very foundation upon which rock 'n' roll was built – music which today is still called 'The Devil's Music'.

Above: Robert Johnson, king of the Delta blues singers.

ROCK AROUND THE

THE TEENAGE REVOLUTION

Before the end of World War II an adolescent growing up was expected to take life very seriously. Men were expected to join the services or get a job and women were expected to marry and have children. The roles were clearly defined and higher education was for the select few. Teenagers had very limited freedom, no economic power and very little influence on the decisions made by their elders. In the 1950s expectations for teenagers changed. Their parents' generation had just gone through a World War which made them acutely aware of the priorities of life. Their families became their main focus. Parents stopped wanting their children to follow the same patterns they had gone through and became more indulgent. Most parents wanted their children to receive a better education. As a result teenagers had access to more money and more free time. They began to have more fun and were less serious than the previous generations. This new, liberal culture began to allow teenagers to make decisions for themselves that often differed from their parents, and their choice of music was very different!

Before World War II a young person's exposure to music was limited. Adults decided what music was allowed in the home and their music was 'white' music like that of Tin Pan Alley. In the 1950s teenagers became more private, clannish, sullen, secretive, defensive and increasingly more disrespectful of their elders. This became what would later be referred to as 'The Generation Gap'. Juvenile delinquency at that time was on the rise and played up by the media. Confused parents thought that eternal damnation was just around the corner, yet the more their choice of music was defamed the more popular it became. With the invention of the transistor radio teenagers could take their music wherever they wanted to.

DJs and radio stations, encouraged by this growing audience, began playing to their listeners' tastes. Jukebox operators and record shops exerted their own influence and teenage choice in music began influencing society. Suddenly teen dress, beliefs, pastimes, social mores and speech patterns differed from those of their parents. Their new music was heard on their radios, on television and at parties. The music was easy to dance to, a feature that appealed to the younger generation. It allowed them to get the energy out of their system and show their athletic prowess. Their dances were a variation of the Lindy or Jitterbug. Slow ballads were included because a fair number of male teens didn't have the confidence or co-ordination to dance fast. A whole industry sprang up to cater to this potentially lucrative market. 'White' teens with more money became the focus of marketing strategies. A new era had begun and it was called rock 'n' roll. The man who brought rock 'n' roll to America and subsequently to the world was, however, not a musician but a disc jockey. His name was Alan Freed.

Above: Teenagers of the 1950s enjoying the new expressive dance style of rock 'n' roll.

MOONDOG'S ROCK 'N' ROLL PARTY

Alan Freed was the DJ who claimed credit for coining the phrase rock 'n' roll. Although the term was used amongst black Americans it was not until 1951 that it was used to describe a genre of music.

Freed was born Albert James Freed in Pennsylvania in 1921 and moved to Salem, Ohio, in 1933. His original ambition was to become a bandleader and he formed his own band in high school called the Sultans of Swing, in which he played trombone. However, due to an ear infection, his plans had to be changed. Whilst attending college he formed an interest in radio and from 1942 began his broadcasting career, first as a sports commentator and then, in 1945, as a DJ playing the latest popular ballads and jazz records.

In 1949 Freed moved to Cleveland, Ohio, and whilst there met Leo Mintz, a local record store owner. Mintz persuaded Freed to play the rhythm and blues records that had seen an upsurge in popularity through the local white teenagers buying them. It was on 11 July 1951 that Alan Freed went on the air at WJW radio as 'Moondog' and became the first DJ to play rhythm and blues for a white teenage audience.

Owing to the stigma in the United States at the time attached to what was a black American form of music and therefore 'race' music, Freed renamed the R&B he played as rock 'n' roll. The Dominoes, a black vocal group, hit the charts in 1951 with their highly suggestive song 'Sixty Minute Man', in which rock 'n' roll is mentioned. It is believed that this inspired Freed a month later to use the term, although it is somewhat ironic that in trying to make it more acceptable he used a slang term for sex.

Moondog's Rock 'n' Roll Party, the name used by Freed for his show became extremely successful. In 1952 he booked the top black acts of the time for his Moondog Coronation Ball to be held at the 10,000-capacity Cleveland Arena. A significant proportion of the audience was white. Unfortunately, thousands tried to gatecrash their way into the already full venue resulting in the dance being cancelled.

In 1954 Freed was hired by WINS radio in New York and moved there. Again, his show rose in popularity and again Freed promoted black R&B performers as rock 'n' roll artists, both on the radio and at revues. The music industry was soon advertising 'rock 'n' roll' records in the trade papers, especially when Freed got the chance to broadcast nationally on CBS. Films soon headed his way and he appeared in five teen rock 'n' roll movies including *Rock Around The Clock*. Strangely, Freed was already in his 30s and yet still managed to appeal to the target audience. He was given his own nationally televised show on ABC TV in 1957. This allowed Freed to bring rock 'n' roll to an even wider audience but when Frankie Lymon (of Frankie Lymon and the Teenagers), a black artist, was seen dancing on screen with a white girl the show was cancelled. ABC had affiliates in the South and this spectacle was deemed an outrage. Further problems hampered Freed's career from there on. In 1958 he was charged with incitement to riot after violence broke out at a show in the Boston Arena. The charges were dropped but not before WINS refused to renew Freed's contract. At this Freed declared himself bankrupt.

He moved to another radio station, WABC, as well as hosting a locally televised music show but in 1959 was fired after being investigated by the US House Oversight Committee. He was under suspicion of accepting bribes, or payola, from record companies in order to play their records. In 1960 eight men, including Freed, were charged with accepting illegal gratuities, further leading to Freed being charged with tax evasion. When he eventually pleaded guilty his career was effectively over. He managed further brief stints as a DJ but his drinking habits took their toll. Following a further indictment by a federal grand jury, again for tax evasion, Alan Freed entered a hospital with complications caused by his drinking. On 20 January 1965 the man who had coined the name rock 'n' roll and brought it to the masses died.

ROCK 'N' ROLL STYLES

During the 1950s four distinct styles of rock 'n' roll began to evolve out of the blues styles:

COUNTRY BOOGIE ALSO CALLED ROCKABILLY

NEW ORLEANS DANCE BLUES, ALSO KNOWN AS DELTA BLUES

CHICAGO URBAN BLUES

VOCAL GROUPS ALSO KNOWN AS DOO-WOP

MEMPHIS, TENNESSEE – COUNTRY BOOGIE

This style was epitomised by Elvis Presley, the most commercially successful of a number of Memphis artists. It is also called rockabilly. These bands played country and western music, cowboy songs, ballads and dance tunes that were being broadcast on the emerging country radio stations of the south-east. Bill Haley, the first exponent of this style of rock 'n' roll, began experimenting by adding old-style rhythm and blues to his catalogue of showband songs.

Above: Elvis, about to cast off his 'hillbilly cat' image.

BIOGRAPHY:

Haley's Comets

Bill Haley and his Comets fused elements of country music, western swing and black R&B to produce some of rock 'n' roll's earliest hits. His 'Crazy Man Crazy' from 1953 was the first white rock 'n' roll record to make the pop charts.

Bill Haley was born in Highland Park, Michigan, in 1925. His father played the mandolin and banjo. He received his first guitar at the age of 13 and his father taught him how to play the basic chords and notes. Although he could not read music he had an ear for country music and was able to pick out any tune he wanted by ear.

Haley left school in June 1940, just before his 15th birthday. He went to work bottling spring water for the sum of 35 cents an hour.

He made his first record, 'Candy Kisses' at the age of 18. For the next four years he sang and played guitar with country and western bands, touring with outfits such as the Down Homers. In September 1946 Haley returned to his parents' home after becoming disillusioned with life on the road. He was sick and penniless and after arriving went to bed for 30 hours straight. His mother nursed her son back to health. Realising that he was not going to make it as a cowboy singer, he left the Down Homers and went to work as the host of a local radio programme.

In 1947 he was hired as musical director for radio station WPWA. He worked 12 to 16 hours a day, six days a week, interviewing a myriad of local people, always looking for good ideas and new talent. On Sundays he would go to Radio Park and interview celebrities, asking them to sing or play their latest songs on a special half-hour programme slot. It was during this time that he put together a band, the Four Aces of Swing, that performed on his show. In 1948, on the Cowboy label, Haley recorded with them. Although they disbanded in mid-49 Haley soon formed a new band, the Saddlemen, with whom he recorded country music.

In the summer of 1950, through the efforts of Jimmy Myers, Bill Haley and his Saddlemen cut their first records. They were on a small Philadelphia independent publisher label called Ed Wilson's Keystone. The songs were ordinary western swing tunes: 'Deal Me A Hand'/'Ten Gallon Stetson' and 'Susan Van Dusan / 'I'm Not To Blame'. These were the first recordings of the band that would become the nucleus of the world-famous Comets.

Bob Johnson, Program Director at WPWA, suggested the name Haley's Comets in deference to their new sound. The Saddlemen changed their image accordingly, removing their boots and stetsons. Bill Haley and his Comets exploded into action. Their song 'Rock the Joint' sold 75,000 copies and in 1953 'Crazy Man Crazy' reached the *Billboard* Top 20 pop chart becoming the first rock 'n' roll record to do so.

On 1 April 1954 Bill Haley signed an unprecedented contract with Decca Records in New York. It was for four records a year, a standard royalty of 5% of sales, $5,000.00 in advance royalties, and the understanding that Decca would mail out each release to 2,000 disc jockeys with full support publicity, including full page ads in *Billboard* and *Cash Box* magazines.

Above: Bill Haley, with guitar, looks on as his Comets erupt.

Eleven days later, at Pythian Temple Studio, Bill Haley recorded 'Rock Around the Clock', the song that introduced rock 'n' roll to the world. In fact it had originally been recorded by Sunny Dae in 1952. Haley's version of 'Rock Around the Clock' had initial sales around 75,000, a modest amount until sales rocketed after it was used in *The Blackboard Jungle*, a movie about juvenile delinquents, some 12 months later. His next record, 'Shake, Rattle and Roll', was a Top 10 hit and was the first rock 'n' roll record to sell a million copies. The next really big hit came with 'See You Later Alligator' which sold a million within a month.

In 1957, Haley began touring Britain as his popularity began to wane at home. He was the first American rock 'n' roll star to come to Britain and was greeted with large and enthusiastic crowds. The reason his popularity with the American teenagers was fading was soon apparent. He was overweight and considered old at 30, compared to his audience. He also had competitors in the form of Little Richard, Jerry Lee Lewis, Gene Vincent and – especially – Elvis Presley. They were younger and their music was more exciting. Although Bill Haley and his Comets were the progenitors they were now part of the establishment.

After 1957 Haley had a few minor hits, but spent the remainder of his life touring and playing rock 'n' roll revival shows. He died in his sleep in the early-morning hours of 9 February 1981 at his home in Harlingen, Texas.

Without the recording studios, the early stars would never have achieved the public recognition that they did. The most important studio for country boogie rock 'n' roll was run by producer (and owner of Sun Records) Sam Phillips.

BIOGRAPHY:
Sam Phillips

In 1950 Sam Phillips, a former radio announcer, rented space at 706 Union Avenue, Memphis, Tennessee, for his Memphis Recording Service and thus began the saga of Sun Records. As a producer, label owner and talent scout, Phillips pioneered a new style of music called rockabilly. The Sun Records label was an early home to Jerry Lee Lewis, Johnny Cash, Roy Orbison, Carl Perkins, Howlin' Wolf and many more of rock 'n' roll's greatest talents. Sun produced more rock 'n' roll records than any other label of its time, including 226 singles. Sam Phillips also discovered Elvis Presley. Sun was responsible for the songs that served as the bedrock of rock 'n' roll, such as Elvis Presley's first five singles (beginning with 'That's All Right'/'Blue Moon of Kentucky' in 1954), Carl Perkins' 'Blue Suede Shoes', Johnny Cash's 'I Walk The Line' and Jerry Lee Lewis' 'Whole Lotta Shakin' Going On'.

Sun was also responsible for Bill Justis' aptly titled sax instrumental 'Raunchy' which hit the Top 3 in the national charts; some of Roy Orbison's earliest recordings, including 'Ooby Dooby'; Billy Lee Riley's 'Flying Saucers Rock and Roll', 'Lonely Weekends' for pianist Charlie Rich and high-charting R&B entries such as Rufus Thomas' 'Bear Cat'. It is a testimony to Phillips' exciting vision of American music that a song like 'Breathless' by Jerry Lee Lewis could hit the Top 10 on the pop, country and black R&B charts alike. Without Sam Phillips' dedication to and promotion of the music we would never have heard of Elvis the Pelvis!

Above: Sun Records founder and pioneer rock 'n' roll producer Sam Phillips.

BIOGRAPHY:

Elvis Presley

Elvis Presley, the undisputed king of rock 'n' roll, was born in Tupelo, Mississippi, in 1935. He grew up listening to the sound of gospel music at the local Pentecostal church and then in 1948, after his family moved to Memphis, was exposed to jazz and blues. After graduating from high school in 1953, an 18-year-old Presley visited the Memphis Recording Service to record his voice. Sam Phillips, impressed by the plaintive emotion in Presley's vocals, teamed him up with bassist Bill Black and guitarist Scotty Moore.

In July 1954 the trio worked on two up-tempo songs, the bluesy 'That's All Right' and the country 'Blue Moon of Kentucky'. Soon, following five groundbreaking singles, Presley's recording contract was sold to RCA Records and his career quickly soared. His last single for Sun and his first one for RCA ,'I Forgot to Remember to Forget', hit No 1 in the country charts, swiftly followed by 'Heartbreak Hotel' which hit all the US charts, reaching No 1 again but this time for eight weeks.

He appeared on national TV variety shows, generating mass hysteria and controversy. White, middle-class, puritanical America was horrified: his hip-thrusting was overtly sexual and it was the first time that a white man had danced like a black man. The teenage audience loved Elvis the Pelvis, though, and he had a number of major hits through 1956 and 1957 including 'Hound Dog', 'Don't Be Cruel', 'Love Me Tender', 'Jailhouse Rock' and 'All Shook Up'

In the 1960s he followed a two-year army stint in Germany with film-making, soundtrack-recording and albums of sacred songs, such as 'How Great Thou Art'.

On 3 December 1968 Presley rejuvenated his standing as a rock 'n' roller with a TV special called *Elvis*. His mid-career renaissance produced some of his most mature and satisfying work. At American Studio in Memphis he cut classic tracks such as 'In the Ghetto', 'Kentucky Rain' and 'Suspicious Minds' with the soulful, down-home musicians there. Indeed he holds records for having 107 Top Forty hits, 38 Top 10 hits, 10 consecutive No 1 hits and 80 weeks at No 1.

In the 1970s Elvis undertook took constant tours, and performed at filled-to-capacity venues all across the US. On 16 August 1977, at the age of 42, King Presley died of a heart attack at Graceland, his Memphis mansion.

Another of Sam Phillips' protegés was Jerry Lee Lewis, the ultimate wild man of rock 'n' roll.

Above: Elvis Presley – jailhouse rocker.

BIOGRAPHY:

Jerry Lee Lewis

Jerry Lee Lewis was brought up to play piano by ear, his first influences being the country-blues sound of Jimmie Rodgers and the gospel and R&B of the local black community in Ferriday, Louisiana. He moved to Memphis, taking his cocktail of playing styles and his rebellious temperament to Sam Phillips' Sun Records label. There he performed what he himself referred to as 'the Devil's music'. He combined an aggressive, up-tempo boogie instrumental style with raucous, uninhibited vocals.

His debut single was 'Crazy Arms' a rocking cover of a country hit. In 1957 his follow-ups 'Whole Lotta Shakin' Going On' and 'Great Balls of Fire' sold six million copies and five million copies respectively. In 1958 he appeared in a film entitled *High School Confidential*, releasing a hit song of the same name and another hit, 'Breathless'. Always one to court controversy, he fell from grace spectacularly when the press discovered he had married his 13-year-old cousin. He managed to continue as a country-music artist with hits such as 'What Made Milwaukee Famous (Made a Loser Out of Me)' and 'Another Place, Another Time' and in the 1980s re-launched his rock 'n' roll career.

In 1957 another young legend-to-be with a totally different appearance to the other wild men of rock 'n' roll arrived on the scene. Buddy Holly was a star of rock 'n' roll for only two short years, but the wealth of material he recorded in that time made a major and lasting impact on popular rock music. He was truly an innovator, writing his own material, and was among the first to exploit advanced studio techniques such as double-tracking. He pioneered and popularised the now-standard rock-band line-up of two guitars, bass and drums. In his final months, he even experimented with orchestration.

PAY LESS AT JERRY LEE LEWIS MUSIC TRUCK
RECORDS AT WHOLESALE... OR NEARLY

Above: The Ferriday Fireball in full flight.

BIOGRAPHY:

Buddy Holly

Buddy Holly was born Charles Hardin Holley in Lubbock, Texas, in 1936. He learned to play guitar, fiddle and piano at an early age. After high school, he formed the Western and Bop Band, a country-oriented act that performed regularly on a local radio station and opened for acts that came through town. He was signed to Decca in 1956 after being spotted by a talent scout, and recorded demos and singles for the label in Nashville under the name Buddy Holly and the Three Tunes. Back in Lubbock, Holly opened a show at the local youth centre for Elvis Presley, an event that accelerated his conversion from country and western to rock 'n' roll.

On 25 February 1957, Holly and a revised band line-up, now dubbed the Crickets, recorded 'That'll Be the Day' at producer Norman Petty's Clovis, New Mexico, studio. This effortless, upbeat track won them a contract with the Coral and Brunswick labels. Later that year it became a No 1 pop hit and reached No 2 on the R&B charts. The terms of Holly's arrangement with his record labels, negotiated by producer/manager Petty, were somewhat unusual. Releases alternated on Brunswick and Coral, with those on the former label credited to Buddy Holly and the latter to the Crickets. Between August 1957 and August 1958, Holly and the Crickets had seven Top 40 singles.

In October 1958, Holly split both with the Crickets and with Petty, moving to Greenwich Village and marrying Maria Elena Santiago. Because of legal and financial problems following his break-up with Petty, Holly reluctantly agreed to join the Winter Dance Party, a bus tour of the Midwest, in the winter of 1959. After a show in Clear Lake, Iowa, Holly chartered a private plane to the next stop on the tour which was Moorhead, Minnesota. Two other performers, Ritchie Valens and the Big Bopper, joined him. Their plane left Mason City, Iowa, airport and crashed immediately after takeoff, killing all aboard.

Holly's catalogue of songs includes such classics of the rock 'n' roll canon as 'Rave On', 'That'll Be the Day', 'Oh Boy!', 'Peggy Sue' and 'Maybe Baby'. Though Holly lacked the sexuality of Elvis Presley he was still an engaging, charismatic figure with his trademark black horn-rimmed glasses and vocal hiccup. His creative self-reliance inspired the coming wave of rock 'n' rollers in the 60s. The Beatles and the Hollies were both influenced by Holly, and the Rolling Stones' first major hit was Holly's 'Not Fade Away'. Buddy Holly was only 22 years old at the time of the crash and his shocking death is immortalised in Don McLean's 'American Pie' as 'The day the music died'.

Another rock 'n' roll hero who made a huge impact was neither a singer nor a songwriter, but a guitarist: Duane Eddy.

Above: Buddy Holly, a true innovator.

BIOGRAPHY:

Duane Eddy

Duane Eddy was born in Corning, New York, in 1938. He moved with his family to Phoenix in his early teens. After Lee Hazlewood (later known for his work with Nancy Sinatra), then a local DJ, received a demo tape from Eddy in 1957, he concocted a trademark formula based upon Eddy's unique playing style, that of 'twang'. They blended picking at single-note melodies on the low strings with a turned-up tremolo using studio production techniques that accentuated the bass sound through an echo chamber. It evoked the sound of revved-up hot rods, the very sound of teenage rebellion.

Eddy composed instrumentals using a wide variety of styles but all featuring the distinctive 'twang' production. He soon became the most successful rock instrumentalist with 15 Top 40 hits in the 50s and 60s including 'Cannonball', 'Forty Miles of Bad Road' and 'Rebel Rouser'. Eddy's album titles typically punned on the word twang: *The Twang's the Thang*, *Twistin' and Twangin'*, and *Twangin' Up a Storm!* In the early 60s, Eddy provided theme songs for films ('Because They're Young', 'Pepe') and TV shows ('Peter Gunn', 'The Ballad of Paladin'). He also demonstrated his breadth of style by recording a country album (*Twang – Country*) and cut an album of surf music (*Surfin'*

With Duane Eddy). He even covered Bob Dylan's songs in an instrumental vein (*Duane Eddy Does Bob Dylan*). His hit streak ended abruptly in 1963, as Eddy became another casualty of the Beatles and the British Invasion bands – ironic, since both George Harrison and Paul McCartney were big fans of his.

While the glory years of 1958 to 1963 are long gone, the sound of Duane Eddy's guitar has reverberated through the decades. During the mid-80s Eddy played some club dates in LA and had a brief West Coast tour with Ry Cooder in 1983. In 1986, the British avant-garde instrumental outfit Art of Noise recruited Eddy to perform on a remake of 'Peter Gunn,' which became a Top 10 hit.

Eddy's influence in rock 'n' roll is seminal. A twangy guitar drove Bruce Springsteen's 'Born to Run,' and twang echoes in the work of the Beatles, Creedence Clearwater Revival, Dave Edmunds, Chris Isaak and many more. His first album, *Have 'Twangy' Guitar Will Travel* (a play on one of Bo Diddley's), was the one of the first rock 'n' roll albums to be released in stereo, charting for 82 weeks and yielding five hit singles.

Apart from the rock 'n' roll bands themselves, the greatest innovators were the songwriters, the most prolific being Leiber and Stoller.

Above: Duane Eddy – the Twang's the Thang.

BIOGRAPHY:

Leiber & Stoller

Jerry Leiber and Mike Stoller were both born in 1933. Leiber was the son of Polish Jews and was raised at the edge of Baltimore's black ghetto; Stoller was raised in Queens, learning the basics of blues and boogie-woogie from black kids whilst attending summer camp, even though he had been classically trained. They met in Los Angeles in 1950 and began to write: Leiber acted as the wise-cracking lyricist, while jazz- and R&B-loving Stoller composed the music.

In 1951 the Robins (later becoming the Coasters) recorded one of the duo's early songs, 'That's What the Good Book Says', for Lester Sill's Modern Records. In 1953 they formed their own label, Spark, which released classics like the Robins' 'Riot in Cell Block No 9'. After a string of similar, groundbreaking records, Leiber and Stoller were signed by Atlantic Records to one of the industry's first independent production deals.

They were particularly influential during rock 'n' roll's first decade, beginning with the original recording of 'Hound Dog' in 1953 by Big Mama Thornton and continuing through to the Drifters' 'On Broadway' in 1963.

They have written, arranged and produced some of the most spirited and memorable rock 'n' roll songs, achieving new heights of wit and musical sophistication. Songs include 'Hound Dog' (covered in 1956 by Elvis Presley), 'Love Potion No 9' (the Clovers), 'Kansas City' (Wilbert Harrison), 'On Broadway' (the Drifters), 'Ruby Baby' (Dion) and 'Stand By Me' (Ben E. King). Their vast repertoire includes virtually every major hit by the Coasters (e.g., 'Searchin'', 'Young Blood', 'Charlie Brown', 'Yakety Yak' and 'Poison Ivy'). They also wrote songs specifically for Elvis Presley such as 'Jailhouse Rock', 'Treat Me Nice' and 'You're So Square (Baby I Don't Care)'. In all, Elvis recorded more than 20 of their magical songs, and they even wrote a country and western song, 'Just Tell Her Jim Said Hello', at his request.

In 1964 they decided to follow up their success at Atlantic by setting up their own record label again. Red Bird Records highlighted the girl-group sound. Their unerring ear for talent brought great young producers and songwriters into the Red Bird fold. The company's very first release – 'Chapel of Love', by the Dixie Cups – shot to No 1 in the US, with 11 of the label's next 30 singles reaching the Top 40, an outstanding percentage in the music industry. Red Bird's commercial success was equalled by the quality of the music, including such girl-group classics as the Shangri-Las' 'Leader of the Pack'. They brought stylistic flavour to their story songs, which ranged from sharp-witted, catchy hipster tunes to gentler, romantic ballads.

Above: Leiber was the wise-cracking lyricist to jazz- and R&B-loving Stoller.

WALKING TO NEW ORLEANS –
DELTA BLUES

New Orleans Dance, also referred to as Delta Blues, had many of its musicians eventually moving to Chicago to influence the Chicago Urban Blues style of rock 'n' roll. Its first major influence had the strange name of Professor Longhair.

Above: Professor Longhair – 'a unique force of nature'.

BIOGRAPHY:

Professor Longhair

Henry Roeland Byrd was born in Bogalusa, Louisiana, and lived in New Orleans from the age of two. As a child, he learned how to play on an old piano that had been left in an alley. He seriously began to master the instrument while working at a Civilian Conservation Corps camp in 1937. After a stint in the service during World War II, he returned to New Orleans and began playing at clubs like the Caledonia, a bar just outside the French Quarter. He was called Professor Longhair, the 'Professor' part being an honorary nickname bestowed on New Orleans piano wizards.

Professor Longhair stands as the foremost exponent of New Orleans piano style. His idiosyncratic style is a rhythmic jambalaya reflecting the freewheeling, good-time spirit of the Crescent City. Professor Longhair had soaked up influences from close-at-hand sources – barrelhouse boogie-woogie, Caribbean rhythms like the rumba and the Crescent City's 'second line' parade rhythms – but the way he pieced these elements together is what made his style such a marvel of fluidity and drive.

He first recorded in 1949 and scored his one and only R&B chart hit with 'Bald Head', released on Mercury. He was then signed to Atlantic and began recording with the label's producer/executives, Ahmet Ertegun and Jerry Wexler.

As a vocalist, Professor Longhair was a classic blues shouter. As a pianist, he was a unique force of nature. Longhair remained locally popular as a working

musician from the late 1940s to the early 1960s, rarely leaving New Orleans. He abandoned the music business in 1964 and, after languishing in obscurity, was rediscovered and enlisted to play at the second New Orleans Jazz & Heritage Festival in 1971. His comeback included tours of Europe and albums for major labels as a new generation discovered his inimitable 'mambo-rumba-boogie' style. He remained the patron saint of Jazzfest, closing out the final show each year until his death in 1980. His lasting legacy to a generation of New Orleans pianists is apparent in the playing of Fats Domino, Huey 'Piano' Smith, James Booker, Dr John and Allen Toussaint who straddle the boundaries between rhythm and blues and rock 'n' roll.

One of the warmest characters in rock 'n' roll, known for his smile as well as his playing, was Fats Domino.

BIOGRAPHY:

Fats Domino

Antoine 'Fats' Domino was born into a musical family in New Orleans in 1928, learning to play from his brother-in-law. He was called the 'Fat Man' and put a New Orleans-style spin on rock 'n' roll. He began performing in local honky-tonks while working odd jobs to make ends meet and by 1949 he had become a fixture at the Hideaway Club. That same year he met Dave Bartholomew, who became his long-time producer, bandleader and collaborator, and made his first record. He was a success on the R&B scene but in 1955 hit the rock 'n' roll mainstream with 'Ain't That a Shame', followed by 'Blueberry Hill', 'I'm Walkin'', 'Blue Monday' and 'Walking to New Orleans'.

As a pianist, singer and songwriter he sold more than 65 million records, more than any other 50s-era rocker except Elvis Presley. Between 1950 and 1963, he had 37 Top 40 hits and 59 singles in the R&B charts. While less of an outgoing personality than some of his extroverted contemporaries, Domino exhibited staying power based on the solid musicality of his recordings and live performances.

Perhaps the most outlandish of the New Orleans rock 'n' rollers was Little Richard.

Above: One of the warmest characters in rock 'n' roll was Fats Domino.

BIOGRAPHY:

Little Richard

Richard Penniman was born during the Depression in Macon, Georgia. As a youngster, he soaked up music – blues, country, gospel, vaudeville. He learned to play piano from an equally flamboyant character named Esquerita who also recorded rock 'n' roll for Capitol Records in their early days.

More than any other performer, Little Richard's shows, with his explosive music and charismatic persona, laid the foundation for 50s rock 'n' roll. His frantically-charged piano playing and raspy, shouted vocals on such classics as 'Tutti Frutti', 'Long Tall Sally' and 'Good Golly, Miss Molly' defined the wild side of rock 'n' roll. His frenzied approach to music was fuelled by a genuinely outrageous personality. Onstage, he'd deliver wild, piano-thumping sermons while costumed in sequinned vests, mascara, lipstick and a pompadour hairdo that shook with every thundering beat.

Little Richard first recorded in a bluesy vein in 1951, but it was during his tenure at Specialty Records, beginning in 1955, that he made his mark. He laid down a stunning succession of hits over the next few years, including 'Rip It Up', 'Slippin' and Slidin'', 'Lucille', 'Jenny Jenny' and 'Keep a Knockin''. In 1956 he also appeared in rock 'n' roll-based films such as *Don't Knock the Rock* and *The Girl Can't Help It*.

In 1957 Richard succumbed to the rigors of fame as a result of personal conflicts brought about by his religious upbringing. He abruptly abandoned music to enrol in Bible college. However, he was lured back by the British Invasion in 1964, regaining his popularity as a performer and a living embodiment of the music's 50s roots. He has made successful comebacks in every decade since and remains a living legend.

One of the most enduring musicians of the New Orleans rock 'n' roll scene is Allen Toussaint.

Above: Little Richard, the 'Georgia Peach', at his peak.

BIOGRAPHY:

Allen Toussaint

Allen Toussaint was born and raised in New Orleans. As a producer, arranger, bandleader, songwriter and session musician he prevented New Orleans' old-school R&B traditions from dying out by keeping pace with developments in the rapidly evolving worlds of soul and funk. He came into his own in the studio for the Minit and Instant labels from 1960 to 1963 after serving apprenticeships with artists such as Fats Domino in the 1950s. His multiple talents allowed him to work for such R&B artists as Lee Dorsey, Jessie Hill, Ernie K-Doe and Chris Kenner. Many listeners heard New Orleans-style piano for the first time via Toussaint's playing on Ernie K-Doe's No 1 hit, 'Mother-in-Law'. 'Fortune Teller,' written by Toussaint under a pseudonym and recorded by Benny Spellman, became a live standard among British bands such as the Rolling Stones and the Who.

From 1963 to 1965 Toussaint served in the army, thus interrupting his career. Upon returning to New Orleans, he formed a production company, Sansu, with partner Marshall Sehorn. A string of soul/R&B singles from singer Lee Dorsey followed in 1965 and 1966, including 'Ride Your Pony,' 'Working in a Coal Mine' and 'Holy Cow.'

Toussaint also groomed a quartet of top-drawer New Orleans musicians known as the Meters. They served as the Sansu house band while releasing funky instrumentals under their own name. In 1973, Toussaint and Sehorn built their own Sea-Saint studio, which attracted local musicians like Dr John ('Right Place Wrong Time') and the Neville Brothers, as well as established stars like Paul McCartney, Paul Simon and Robert Palmer. Labelle recorded their 1975 hit 'Lady Marmalade' there.

As a talented pianist and performer in his own right he also recorded under his own name. In 1958 he released an instrumental album, 'The Wild Sound of New Orleans'. His 'Whipped Cream' instrumental served as the title track of the third album by Herb Alpert and the Tijuana Brass, which topped the album chart for eight weeks in 1965. In the 1970s Toussaint recorded three R&B albums for Warner Bros. In addition to his endless production resumé, various Toussaint-penned songs, published under both his own name and the pseudonym Naomi Neville (his mother's maiden name), have been covered by such notables as the Rolling Stones, the Yardbirds, Bonnie Raitt, Boz Scaggs, Little Feat, Herb Alpert and Glen Campbell.

Above: Allen Toussaint — one of the most enduring musicians of the New Orleans rock 'n' roll scene.

SHAKE YOUR MONEYMAKER –
CHICAGO URBAN BLUES

Chuck Berry, Howlin' Wolf, Elmore James, Muddy Waters and Bo Diddley were all well known Chicago-based artists, but it took the Chess brothers, through their recording studio, to bring their music to the masses and so influence a whole generation of rock musicians.

Above: Phil Chess of Chicago's Chess Records.

BIOGRAPHY:

The Chess Brothers

Leonard and Phil Chess founded Chess Records in 1949. The Chess brothers had immigrated from Poland with their family and settled in Chicago. The Chess label released a huge assortment of blues, R&B and rock 'n' roll talent including Muddy Waters, Howlin' Wolf, Chuck Berry, Bo Diddley, Willie Dixon, Etta James and Little Walter. Phil focused on the jazz whilst Leonard concentrated on roots music, making Chess the greatest repository of black music in the 1950s. Leonard Chess died in Chicago in October 1969.

It was under Chess's tutelage that Muddy Waters' electric blues began the musical revolution that inspired Chuck Berry, one of the greatest rock 'n' rollers of all time.

Above: Leonard Chess of Chicago's Chess Records.

BIOGRAPHY:

Chuck Berry

Charles Edward Berry was born in St Louis in October 1926. In the early 50s, Berry led a popular blues trio by night and worked as a beautician by day. He befriended Muddy Waters, who thought highly enough of Berry's ability to introduce him to Leonard Chess. It was not his bluesy numbers that convinced Chess to sign Berry but a song on his audition tape called 'Ida Red,' a fast, R&B-country hybrid that Berry later reworked into 'Maybellene'. Released in August 1955, 'Maybellene' hit No 5 in *Billboard* and established Berry as a rarity – a black artist who successfully crossed over to the white pop charts.

Chuck Berry was the man who put all the essential pieces of rock 'n' roll together, splicing country and western guitar licks onto a rhythm and blues frame

from his very first single. Add to this his rapid-fire lyrics, full of innuendo about cars and girls, and Berry had laid the groundwork for not only a rock 'n' roll sound but a rock 'n' roll attitude. That first single also included a scorching guitar solo built around his trademark double-string licks. Accompanied by long-time piano player Johnnie Johnson and members of the Chess Records house band, including Willie Dixon, Berry wrote and performed timeless rock 'n' roll. The cream of his repertoire including 'Johnny B. Goode,' 'Sweet Little Sixteen,' 'Rock and Roll Music' and 'Roll Over Beethoven', are standards for any would-be guitarist even now.

Berry's songs were essentially about the experience of being a teenager in the changing world of the 50s, whether he was describing the boredom of classroom-bound students in 'School Days' or the liberating appeal of rock 'n' roll itself in 'Rock and Roll Music'.

Berry gave rock 'n' roll an archetypal character in 'Johnny B. Goode' and was responsible for one of its most recognisable stage moves, his famous 'duckwalk'. All the while, his songs – even the lesser-known ones like 'Little Queenie' and 'Let It Rock' – were being mastered by aspiring rockers on the other side of the ocean, such as Keith Richards and John Lennon, with many other British acts also covering them. In 1962 Berry was sentenced to two years in prison on what now appear to be trumped-up charges. After his release he still made some rock 'n' roll classics such as 'No Particular Place to Go', 'You Never Can Tell' and 'Promised Land'. Even groups like the Beach Boys plundered Berry for inspiration: their 1963 hit 'Surfin' USA' so blatantly stole the melody and rhythm of Berry's 'Sweet Little Sixteen' that he sued and won a song-writing credit. His music was so renowned that on tour he was able to recruit his band from local musicians in each new town. Ironically, this pioneer of rock 'n' roll had only one No 1 hit, 'My Ding-a-Ling', a suggestive novelty song he had long been performing in adult night-clubs.

One of Chuck Berry's stablemates at Chess Records created one of the cornerstone rhythms of rock 'n' roll – the Bo Diddley beat.

Above: Chuck Berry, the man who put all the essential pieces of rock 'n' roll together.

BIOGRAPHY:

Bo Diddley

Bo Diddley was born Ellas Bates in McComb, Mississippi. His mother moved to Chicago when he was nine and he was brought up by her cousin, Gussie McDaniel. At the age of ten he was given his first guitar at Christmas. He formed a band at high school and became a working musician in 1951, landing a residency at the 708 Club on Chicago's South Side. In 1955 he signed to the Checker label (a spin-off of brothers Phil and Leonard Chess's Chess Records), becoming a label-mate of Chuck Berry. His debut single was the memorable pairing of 'Bo Diddley' and 'I'm a Man'. Along with that and other classic 45s came a string of albums whose titles (such as *Bo Diddley Is a Gunslinger* and *Have Guitar Will Travel*) bolstered his legend. In concert, Diddley became a regular performer at Harlem's Apollo theatre and also travelled with the rock 'n' roll roadshows of the day.

His distinctive African-based rhythm pattern, the 'Bo Diddley beat', employed in his namesake song 'Bo Diddley' and 'Mona', was picked up by other artists and has been a recurring element in rock 'n' roll ever since. It can be heard on Buddy Holly's 'Not Fade Away', the Who's 'Magic Bus' and Bruce Springsteen's 'She's the One'. Any account of Bo Diddley's career in music must also mention his rectangular 'cigar box' guitar. He designed the uniquely shaped instrument himself, building the first one in 1945 .Moreover, he is the author of a unique body of songs – including 'Who Do You Love?', 'Road Runner', 'You Don't Love Me', and 'I'm a Man' which are among the earliest examples of rock 'n' roll close to its source of rhythm and blues.

Diddley came from two worlds, the delta of Mississippi and the streets of Chicago... as did Muddy Waters.

Above: The mighty Bo Diddley and his famous 'cigar box' guitar.

BIOGRAPHY:

Muddy Waters

Muddy Waters (real name McKinley Morganfield) was born into a sharecropper family on the Mississippi Delta in 1915. While working in the cotton fields on Stovall's Plantation, just outside Clarksdale, Muddy learned to sing, earning a mere 50 cents a day. At the age seven he began to learn the harmonica, but did not learn to play guitar until the age of 17. Thereafter, Muddy began performing with friends at local house parties, meanwhile developing an appreciation for the deep blues sounds that Delta bluesman Son House wrung from his guitar. Muddy fabricated his style from House's music and later borrowed ideas from Robert Johnson.

Muddy Waters was first recorded in 1941, for Alan Lomax. The folklorist was compiling songs for the Library of Congress. Two of the cuts were included on the Library's folk anthology album: 'I Be's Troubled' and 'Country Blues'. Lomax would return to the plantation a year later to lay down more tracks with Muddy.

Muddy Waters left the Mississippi Delta bound for Chicago in 1943. With the help of Big Bill Broonzy, he broke into the city's thriving blues scene. For some time, he played acoustic guitar behind John Lee 'Sonny Boy' Williamson. In 1944 he began his assault on the electric guitar. This is when his reputation as a performer took shape. At this time he was still devoted to the traditional Delta bottleneck style, but his sound was fatter, louder, and far more moving than before.

His initial recordings in Chicago were for producer Lester Melrose and Columbia Records in 1946. They featured Muddy with a five-piece band. A year later

he played in support of Sunnyland Slim on two sides titled 'Johnson Machine Gun' and 'Fly Right Little Girl'. In 1948 Muddy recorded 'I Can't Be Satisfied' and 'Feel Like Going Home' in a traditional Delta blues style. His shivering guitar licks provided an exciting new edge to the session. Released by Chess as an Aristocrat single, the record sold out in less than a day.

What ensued in the years 1951 to 1960 was the creation of the greatest collection of electric blues recordings ever produced, defining the Chicago blues style during this classic period. Waters originals like 'Long Distance Call', 'Mannish Boy', 'Got my Mojo Working', 'She Loves Me', and 'She's Nineteen Years Old' were complemented by songs by Willie Dixon such as 'Hoochie Coochie Man', 'I Just Want to Make Love to You', and 'I'm Ready' among others. Muddy's recordings and performances were equipped with extraordinary power by his thick and rough voice. By this point, though, he had stopped playing the guitar.

Chess Records released his debut album in 1958, a collection of hit singles entitled *The Best of Muddy Waters*. That same year he and his pianist, Otis Spann, embarked on a tour of England. These new audiences seemed to prefer the acoustic rural-flavoured blues, as opposed to the riveting electric style that Muddy perfected in the 50s.

Muddy Waters injected electricity into the blood of his new folk-blues audience at the Newport Folk Festival in 1960. He and his high-wattage band performed a fiery set that resulted in the live album *Muddy Waters at Newport*. This created a demand for the electric blues not only from those who attended the festival but from new blues fans everywhere.

To capitalise on this new audience, Chess Records continued to promote Muddy as a folk-blues artist in the 60s. But towards the end of that decade and in the dawn of the new, he released the electrified *Fathers and Sons*, *They Call Me Muddy Waters*, and *The London Muddy Waters Sessions*.

The 1970s saw the end of Muddy's association with Chess Records and a resurgence in his recording career. Signing with CBS/Blue Sky and his collaboration with producer-guitarist Johnny Winter resulted in Muddy's second Grammy, for *Hard Again* in 1977. Non-stop touring brought his music to audiences around the world. A US tour included performances at the White House for President Jimmy Carter as well as an exceptional performance of 'Mannish Boy' captured in *The Last Waltz*, the filmed documentary of the Band's farewell concert . Muddy continued to create with Johnny Winter, enjoying both critical and commercial success, and the two would perform together into the early 1980s.

The majority of their audiences were white blues or rock fans who came to pay homage.

Muddy's final public performance occurred, suitably, at an Eric Clapton show in 1982. He died of a heart attack in 1983.

Another former plantation worker was Howlin' Wolf.

Above: From plantation to the White House – the electrifying Muddy Waters.

BIOGRAPHY:

Howlin' Wolf

Howlin' Wolf was born Chester Arthur Burnett on a Mississippi plantation in 1910. He picked up his nickname 'Howlin' Wolf' in his youth. From an early age he listened to the blues through performers such as Charley Patton and Willie Brown, who performed at plantation picnics and juke joints. Wolf derived his trademark howl from the 'blue yodel' of country singer Jimmie Rodgers, whom he admired. Although he sang the blues locally, it wasn't until he moved to Memphis in 1948 that he put together a full-time band. As a singer he was electrifying, with gruff, rasping vocals, embodying the blues at its most primal. He fully utilised his imposing size, weighing nearly 300 pounds and standing over six feet tall, during his performances.

Producer Sam Phillips recorded Howlin' Wolf at his Memphis Recording Service (later Sun Records) after hearing him perform on radio station KWEM. Some of the material was leased to Chess Records, and in the early 1950s Howlin' Wolf signed with Chess and moved to Chicago, remaining there until his death. He recorded some of his greatest works there, many of which were written by Willie Dixon, such as 'Back Door Man', 'Little Red Rooster' and 'I Ain't Superstitious'. Wolf was also a very capable songwriter, responsible for such classics as 'Killing Floor', 'Smokestack Lightning' and 'Moanin' at Midnight'.

Howlin' Wolf influenced such blues-based rock musicians as the Rolling Stones and Eric Clapton. In the early 1970s he recorded a pair of albums – *The London Howlin' Wolf Sessions* and *London Revisited* – with his British disciples. Wolf's distinctive vocal style and ferocious approach to the blues can also be heard in the work of such diverse artists as Captain Beefheart and his Magic Band and Led Zeppelin. Sadly, following a car accident in which he sustained serious internal injuries, Howlin' Wolf gave his last performance in Chicago in November 1975 with fellow blues star B.B. King. He died of kidney failure two months later.

Although not a member of the Chess stable, Elmore James is a musician whose influence is still heard today.

Above: Howlin' Wolf derived his trademark howl from the 'blue yodel' of Jimmie Rodgers.

BIOGRAPHY:

Elmore James

Elmore James was born on a farm in Richland, Mississippi, in 1918. It was fellow bluesman, Robert Johnson's local performances that inspired him to take up the guitar. He travelled the South, often performing alongside Sonny Boy Williamson during the 1930s and 1940s. In 1953 he moved to Chicago, where he participated in the birth and blossoming of electric blues. He spent the next decade bobbing back and forth between Chicago and Mississippi, making a detour to New York City in 1959 to record for the Fire label.

James' signature tune, 'Dust My Broom' by Robert Johnson, formed the foundation of his recording career. James first cut a cover of it in August 1951, playing the swooping, full-octave opening figure on slide guitar. He has been credited with inventing blues rock by virtue of his primal riffs and driving intensity.

James died of a heart attack in Chicago in 1963, leaving behind a raft of classic blues songs that include 'Shake Your Moneymaker', 'Talk to Me Baby', 'It Hurts Me Too' and 'The Sky Is Crying'. His distinctive style has influenced a legion of slide players ever since, his songs having been covered by the Allman Brothers, Fleetwood Mac, Canned Heat and the Butterfield Blues Band.

Above: Elmore James has been credited with inventing blues rock.

DOO-WOP DOO-WOP – VOCAL GROUPS

This style evolved from the doo-wop acapella style of the Orioles and the Coasters, through Frankie Lymon and the Teenagers, eventually culminating in Phil Spector's productions of the Ronettes during the early 60s.

Above: The Coasters were among the most popular music groups in America.

BIOGRAPHY:

The Coasters

A black vocal group called the Robins formed in Los Angeles in 1947. They signed to Leiber and Stoller's label, Spark Records, in the early 1950s and recorded some notable R&B records, including 'Riot in Cell Block No 9' and 'Smokey Joe's Café'. In 1955, Atlantic Records offered Leiber and Stoller and the Robins a deal with Atco, a subsidiary label. Several members stayed in Los Angeles and continued as the Robins but bass singer Bobby Nunn and tenor Carl Gardner headed to New York City, where they recruited tenor Leon Hughes and baritone Billy Guy. The new group called themselves the Coasters, alluding to their coast-to-coast relocation. The classic Coasters line-up solidified with the addition of tenor Cornell Gunter and bass Will 'Dub' Jones, who replaced Hughes and Nunn.

The Coasters recorded a string of rhythm and blues hits sung in an infectious, up-tempo doo-wop style. The group sang Leiber and Stoller-penned songs including such classics as 'Yakety Yak', 'Charlie Brown', 'Along Came Jones' and 'Poison Ivy'. During their late-50s heyday, the Coasters' recordings were accompanied by honking sax solos from King Curtis.

In 1957, the Coasters reached No 1 on the R&B charts and the pop Top 10 with their double-sided single 'Searchin'' and 'Young Blood'. Over the next two years, the Coasters had a series of hit singles, all filled with New York street slang and timeless rock 'n' roll humour. By the end of the 1950s, they ranked among the most popular musical groups in America inspiring, amongst others, Frankie Lymon and the Teenagers.

Frankie Lymon and the Teenagers

Frankie Lymon was born in New York City in 1942. He was working in a grocery store when he met a group of neighbourhood singers, the Premiers. Having sung gospel music in his father's group, the pre-teen Lymon easily made the transition to secular music. The Premiers renamed themselves the Teenagers with Lymon singing the high parts in his clear, pure boy soprano.

'Why Do Fools Fall in Love?' was recorded for Gee Records late in 1955 and released in early 1956. It reached No 1 in the UK and was the No 1 R&B hit in the US when Frankie Lymon was only 13. The song has attained the status of a vocal-group classic, owing to Lymon's agile, ingenuous and utterly charming performance with the doo-wopping Teenagers, and is one of the key records by which the doo-wop style is defined and remembered. Its success allowed Lymon to become the first black teenage pop star, serving as an example for such 60s child stars as Michael Jackson and Little Stevie Wonder.

Launched into instant stardom by the success of 'Why Do Fools Fall in Love?' (formerly titled 'Why Do Birds Sing So Gay?'), the group suddenly found themselves in movies and on tours at home and overseas. In 1956 and 1957, five other singles by Frankie Lymon and the Teenagers made the R&B Top Ten – including 'I Want You to Be My Girl', 'Who Can Explain?' and 'The ABCs of Love' although the group never entered the US pop charts again. Sadly, Lymon's star fell as quickly as it rose, and he was found dead of a heroin overdose in February 1968. He was only 25 years old. Although Frankie Lymon and the Teenagers didn't leave behind a huge body of work, their handful of hits still rank among the finest recordings from the golden era of rock 'n' roll.

Many people believe that the seminal vocal group of this time were the Everly Brothers.

Above: Frankie Lymon and the Teenagers – their hits still rank as the finest from the golden era of rock 'n' roll.

BIOGRAPHY:

The Everly Brothers

Phil and Don Everly were the sons of entertainers Margaret and Ike Everly, a travelling country and western team. They first performed as part of the family act on radio and in concert. On their own they transformed the Appalachian folk, bluegrass and country sounds of their Kentucky boyhood into a richly harmonised form of rock 'n' roll with melancholic ballads of youthful romance in clear, dreamy voices. With Don taking the melody and Phil harmonising above him, the Everlys released a string of hit records between 1957 and 1962 that managed to cross over from country to pop, even entering the black R&B charts.

The duo rose to prominence on the New York-based Cadence label, recording songs written for them by the husband and wife team of Felice and Boudleaux Bryant. The Bryants wrote and the Everlys sang eloquently of teenage devotion and heartbreak. The Bryant-penned Everlys hits include such timeless favourites as 'Bye Bye Love', 'Wake Up Little Susie', 'Devoted to You', 'Bird Dog', 'Poor Jenny' and 'All I Have to Do Is Dream'. The brothers also became accomplished songwriters, writing such original hits as 'Cathy's Clown', 'When Will I Be Loved' and '('Til) I Kissed You'.

In 1960 they signed a 10-year contract with Warner Brothers and recorded prolifically during the following decade. Even though the hits stopped flowing in 1962, the Everly Brothers' influence continued to spread. Their close-harmony singing directly influenced a rising tide of musicians that included the Beatles, the Hollies, Simon & Garfunkel, and the Byrds. In 1973 the duo had an acrimonious break-up, but in 1983 resolved their differences at a reunion concert at London's Royal Albert Hall. Subsequently, they resumed their partnership onstage and in the studio.

Rock 'n' roll produced a huge number of different performers and styles. The one thing they have in common is the instrument that backed them up – the electric guitar.

Above: The Everly Brothers sang of teenage devotion and heartbreak.

Guitar men –
The History of the Electric Solid-Body Guitar

The electric guitar owes its existence to the popularity of Hawaiian music in the 1920s and 1930s. Hawaiian guitars were solo instruments played with a metal slide. Electric Hawaiian guitars were the first instruments that depended entirely on their sound being amplified electrically rather than just acoustically.

Adolph Rickenbacker, who originally made metal components for Dopera Brothers' National Resonator Guitars, met George Beauchamp and Paul Barth who had been working on the principle of the magnetic pick-up. They formed the Electro String Company and in 1931 produced their first electric Hawaiian guitars. Their success prompted other companies to start producing their own electric guitars.

During the 1940s Gibson's new electric Hawaiian guitars became firmly established and are still one of the most popular today. In 1944, Leo Fender, a radio repair specialist, and Doc Kaufman, a former Rickenbacker employee, started K & F Company. They produced a series of steel guitars and amplifiers. Fender felt the large pick-up magnets in use at the time did not need to be so big. He designed a smaller pick-up to put into a solid-body guitar based on the Hawaiian shape but with a properly fretted fingerboard. Although meant as a demonstration model, the guitar was soon in demand. In 1946 the Fender Electric Instrument Company was formed and the Broadcaster, later renamed the Telecaster, was put into production. In 1954 Fender began producing the Stratocaster alongside the Telecaster.

At the same time, Les Paul, inspired by a solid-body violin made by Thomas Edison, began experimenting with pick-ups in a solid-body guitar in order to reduce feedback problems. He persuaded Epiphone to let him use their workshop, where in 1941 he built the historic 'log' guitar. He later joined forces with Gibson to produce the famous Gibson 'Les Paul' signature guitars that all wannabe rock stars dream of owning – the ultimate teenage dream.

As the teenage revolution swept the USA, across the pond in Great Britain the same feelings were beginning to stir. In America it was the soda bar that became the hangout for teenagers; in Britain it was the coffee bar.

Expresso Bongo –
rock 'n' roll in the 1950s in the UK

Post-war Britain during the 1950s was a drab and grey place. There was still rationing and there were no 'teenagers'. The first stirrings of what was to become the teenage phenomenon came when urban working-class boys looked for a new identity. They chose a strange Edwardian style of fashion, wearing long high-neck drape jackets, sometimes of velvet, which were lined with bright paisley colours. These were worn with brocade waistcoats, boot-lace ties, narrow, drainpipe trousers, wing-collared shirts and suede shoes. As essential accessories they carried bicycle chains (for fighting)

and combs. They used the combs frequently as their Tony Curtis-type hairstyles, called the bop or the DA, were liberally greased with 'Brylcreem' and were easily messed up in a fight. They called themselves Teddy Boys. They hung around in gangs, particularly in south London. In the dance halls they jived to be-bop music, a remnant from the American bands who had played here during the war. The association between these youths, their dance music, their clothes and crime had already become a major source of concern by 1954 when a gang of Teds murdered a youth on Clapham Common.

Above: Saturday Club's Brian Matthew also hosted the TV show Thank Your Lucky Stars.

Unlike America, where teenagers could listen to rock 'n' roll and blues music on their local radio stations, Britain at this time only had two music stations – the BBC Light Programme and the BBC Home Service. By an arrangement with the Musicians' Union the BBC had a limited allocation of time for playing recorded music. Most of its airtime was devoted to a selection of radio dramas, comedy shows and opinion panels. Its live music shows ranged from cinema organ sessions through palm court trios and popular music. The popular music was largely American but of the white, clean-cut ballads type. The exception to this was a radio show, *Saturday Club*, that began in 1958 and was hosted by Brian Matthew. This programme had a unique format, mixing live singers and pop records with interviews and a commentary from the presenter. There were also two alternative radio stations that could be listened to: Radio Luxembourg, a commercial station based on the continent which was sponsored by American record companies and so allowed early US rock 'n' roll to be heard; and *American Forces Network,* which also played American chart hits.

The other information that teenagers were able to gather about their music was from the *New Musical Express,* which instigated Britain's first official 'Hit Parade' in 1952. However, this chart was really just a copy of the songs listed in *Billboard* in the US.

In 1954 Bill Haley's 'Shake, Rattle and Roll' and 'Rock Around the Clock' were released in the UK and for many people these were the first records of their kind that they had ever heard. They became major hits and then the movie *Rock Around the Clock* hit the cinemas This provoked audiences in some areas to rip out the seats in order to give themselves room to jive. Dance halls at the time played strict-tempo ballroom dancing

music and youth clubs tended to be run by religious groups. Rock 'n' roll changed all that. Now teenagers demanded that their own music was played in as many places as possible and a new phenomenon appeared called the espresso coffee bar. In these coffee bars were jukeboxes, filled with the hits of the day, both American and British. Some of them, at times, had live music playing. The most famous of these was the 2 I's Coffee Bar in Soho, London. It was here that Britain's new beat generation was born.

But before rock 'n' roll hit town, another musical fad took Britain by storm. It was called skiffle, and the King of Skiffle was Lonnie Donegan. He inspired a whole generation of young men to find instruments and go out into the world and make music.

Lonnie Donegan

Anthony James Donegan was born in Glasgow in 1931 to Scots–Irish parents. He taught himself to play guitar at 14 and formed his own outfit, the Tony Donegan Jazz Band. A turning point came when he was booked at the Royal Festival Hall as support to American Blues singer Lonnie Johnson. The show's compere mistakenly introduced 'Tony Donegan' as 'Lonnie Donegan' and he adopted the name from then on.

Later Donegan co-founded the Chris Barber Jazzband, playing guitar and banjo but also performing vocal 'skiffle sessions' at live concerts. Although singing was secondary to him, ironically it was his version of 'Rock Island Line' on their first album that attracted the radio plays. Decca Records released it as a single, resulting in Donegan being plucked from the band by Pye Records and whisked off to the USA for his first solo appearance on the Perry Como TV Show.

Lonnie had many UK chart hits alongside Presley until the Mersey Sound took over the record market. He had little choice but to switch his act to suit cabaret audiences around the world's top nightspots. He spent the late 60s and most of the 70s starring in 'seasons' at such places as Las Vegas, New York, London and Hollywood.

By the early 80s, theatres were reclaiming their audiences and there was a renewed demand for the King of Skiffle in Britain. Although not strictly rock 'n' roll his influence cannot be emphasised enough. Without him there would be no Beatles or Rolling Stones or any of the earlier British rockers.

When the American rock 'n' roll shows began touring the UK and people began buying records by Presley, Jerry Lee Lewis and other rock 'n' rollers, the British music industry attempted to exploit this. An impresario in London called Larry Parnes began to produce a host of singers with cartoon-like names who became the UK's equivalent to rock 'n' roll. The first was Tommy Steele, who was more of a music-hall style entertainer, followed by Marty Wilde and the Wildcats (who covered US rock 'n' roll hits) and Billy Fury who set a precedent by writing some of his 19 Top 20 hits himself. The most accomplished and successful British singer was Cliff Richard who modelled his style and image on Presley. Cliff Richard made a number of Top 10 singles and starred in British-made films of the time. He was by no means a rock 'n' roller in the true sense, though. He was and still is a clean-cut boy with no bad habits, the complete antithesis of the spirit of rock 'n' roll.

Almost all of the British rock 'n' roll records until 1962 were soulless, mainly because the young 'pretty' boy vocalists were accompanied by musicians who had no feelings for the rhythms of rock 'n' roll. Meanwhile, in the darkest depths of Liverpool, a skiffle group called the Quarrymen were about to change the world.

Above: Lonnie Donegan.

THE SWINGING 60S

Above: Queueing for the Cavern.

ARE YOU EXPERIENCED? ROCK 'N' ROLL IN THE UK IN THE EARLY 1960S

On 16 January 1957, in a basement at No 10 Matthew Street, Liverpool, alternative live music was born in the UK. That was the day the Cavern Club opened for the first time. On the bill that night were a 'skiffle' group and three jazz bands. Little did they, or the audience, know that this was to become the 20th century's most famous nightclub. The Cavern was created by Alan Sinter who owned two other jazz clubs in Liverpool. He wanted his new club to emulate the French cellar clubs that were so popular on the left bank in Paris. The club held 600 people, but on most nights there were queues around the block. Within three years the Cavern Club's membership was 20,000. Bands came to play there from all over the world and it became a focal point for the UK jazz scene.

Very shortly, skiffle grew more and more popular and the Cavern began to open at lunchtimes. The lunchtime sessions were created to target city-centre workers who would not normally come to this part of town at night. The sessions were a huge success and even attracted schoolchildren through, or despite, a 'no alcohol' policy. After the Cavern was sold at the end of 1959 to Ray McFall a new policy was adopted. Many of its customers were leaving to go to other clubs around town to listen to what was then called 'beat' music. Although McFall hated the music and wanted to keep the Cavern as a jazz club, he began to experiment by allowing beat to be played on Wednesday nights.

The first beat night was headlined by Rory Storm and the Hurricanes on 25 May 1960. By the following year beat had taken over Tuesday nights, some lunchtimes and Wednesdays. Jazz and all its genres were slowly fading in popularity – and then a leather-clad rock 'n' roll band who had just returned from Hamburg made their debut. This band was so successful that they were immediately given three to four lunchtime slots a week as well as playing most weekends. They were so popular that the Cavern had to introduce pre-purchased tickets in order to keep the queues at bay.

Biography:

The Beatles

In 1958 a group variously known as the Quarrymen and Johnny and the Moondogs included Liverpudlians John Lennon, Paul McCartney and George Harrison. With a rhythm section consisting of bassist Stu Sutcliffe and drummer Pete Best, the group assumed the name 'the Silver Beetles'. After performing in many local clubs and bars the band went to Hamburg, Germany, and played at the Star Club in the red-light district, playing five-sets-a-night marathon gigs and honing their performances. Their early repertoire consisted of well-chosen rock 'n' roll and rhythm and blues covers, from Chuck Berry to Little Richard. In April 1961, Sutcliffe left and McCartney changed from guitar to bass. By now the band had changed its name to 'the Beatles'. Back in Liverpool, the group landed their lunchtime residency at the Cavern, where they were discovered by a local record merchant and entrepreneur, Brian Epstein. He became their manager in December 1961.

Epstein smartened up the group's appearance by dressing them in dapper, collarless grey suits, instead of their usual rocker leather look, making them appear more friendly.

Above: Young rockers in Hamburg – Best, Harrison, Lennon, McCartney and Sutcliffe.

After being rejected by Decca Records the Beatles signed with EMI-Parlophone in April 1962, having impressed producer George Martin. In August, Ringo Starr (born Richard Starkey), who'd been drumming with Rory Storm and the Hurricanes, was brought in to replace Pete Best. The group's first single, 'Love Me Do'/'PS I Love You', briefly dented the UK Top 20 in October 1962, but their next 45, 'Please Please Me', ignited Beatlemania by reaching the No Two spot. It was followed by four consecutive chart-topping singles, issued throughout 1963: 'From

Me to You', 'She Loves You', 'I Want to Hold Your Hand' and 'Can't Buy Me Love'. The group's success was based around the Lennon/McCartney song-writing partnership, Harrison's guitar-playing prowess, and Starr's amiability and artful simplicity as a drummer, although their first single made use of a session drummer.

The Beatles' conquest of America early in 1964 launched what was called 'the British Invasion'. The Fab Four's first No 1 single in the US was 'I Want to Hold Your Hand', released on Capitol Records, EMI's American counterpart. This exuberant track was followed by 45 more Top 40 hits over the next half-dozen years. During the week of 4 April 1964, the Beatles set a record that is unlikely to be broken when they occupied all five of the top positions on *Billboard*'s Top Pop Singles chart, with 'Can't Buy Me Love' at No 1. In August 1964 their popularity rocketed further with the release of their playfully anarchic film, *A Hard Day's Night*.

The Beatles had 20 No 1 singles in the States, three more than Elvis Presley. For such huge sales and airplay alone, the Beatles are regarded as the top pop group in rock 'n' roll history. Their significance extends beyond statistics to their innovative recording studio techniques. The Beatles' legacy as a concert attraction, during their harried passage from nightclubs to baseball stadiums, was ruined by both the deafening screams of female fans overcome by the group's appearance and the primitive audio technology of the time. No one before had filled such large stadiums with so many noisy fans and the PA systems were simply unable to cope.

Above: Sgt Pepper's Lonely Hearts Club Band – the first concept album.

This led to PA companies making vast improvements in their equipment, but this came too late for the Beatles and so they began to concentrate on their studio work.

They layered sounds and crafted songs in a way that had not been attempted before, resulting in such musically innovative and lyrically sophisticated albums as *Rubber Soul* and *Revolver*.

In 1967 they released *Sgt Pepper's Lonely Hearts Club Band*, stunning both fans and critics alike. It was a mixture of psychedelic fantasies, music hall frivolity and cosmic humour. It was also the first time that an album had been made as a complete unit – most albums were just a random selection of songs. As such it was the first concept album and attempts have been made to emulate it ever since. This album was not just a watershed for the band but for the whole music industry. It realised the band members' collective creativity, took four months to make and was produced using all the technical prowess of George Martin at EMI's Abbey Road studios. Unusually, no singles were released from it.

After the death of manager Brian Epstein, due to an overdose of sleeping pills, the psychedelic TV film *Magical Mystery Tour* was released and surprisingly slated by the press. The Beatles 'took a trip' to India to meditate with Maharishi Mahesh Yogi, leading Lennon to write the cynical putdown 'Sexy Sadie' and George Harrison to become a member of the Transcendental Meditation movement and help finance the Hari Krishna organisation. In January 1968 Apple Corps Ltd was launched and was so badly mismanaged that the resulting financial chaos took years to sort out.

However, through all the chaotic events of the late 60s, the Beatles managed to retain their artistic integrity and focus as recording artists. Their 1968 single 'Hey Jude'/'Revolution' was their most popular. *The White Album* showed up the singular talents of each band member. The album and film *Let It Be*, released in 1970 documented the Beatles' dissolution amid internal squabbles and the distracting presence of John Lennon's new mate, Yoko Ono. The Beatles worked hard and exited on a high note, uniting in the summer of 1969 to record their swan song, 'Abbey Road'.

On 10 April 1970, Paul McCartney announced his departure from the Beatles, and the group disbanded. Throughout the 70s the group members pursued solo careers with varying degrees of artistic and commercial success. The fans' hopes for a reunion were forever dashed by the murder of John Lennon in New York City in 1980. In 2001 George Harrison died of cancer.

As the Cavern Club in Liverpool became the most famous nightclub in the world, the club in London where rock 'n' roll bands made their debut was called the Marquee and was in Soho. The London rock 'n' roll scene was bluesier in attitude than Liverpool. Whereas Liverpool produced a bevy of bands that exemplified the Mersey Sound, they were more pop groups than rock 'n' roll bands. The Beatles are undisputedly the 'greatest pop group in the world', but in London another band was performing that were to become the 'greatest rock 'n' roll band in the world' and they were called the Rolling Stones.

BIOGRAPHY:

The Rolling Stones

The Rolling Stones' earliest origins date back to the boyhood friendship of Mick Jagger and Keith Richard. This friendship was interrupted when Richard's family moved out of Jagger's neighbourhood to the south of London, but was rekindled a decade later in 1960 when the two ran into each other on a train. Jagger, a student at the London School of Economics, was a hardcore blues aficionado, while Richard's interest leaned more toward Chuck Berry-style rock 'n' roll. Richard soon joined Jagger's group, 'Little Boy Blue and the Blue Boys'.

While making the rounds of London's blues clubs, Jagger and Richard befriended guitarist Brian Jones, a member of Blues Incorporated which was led by Alexis Korner, a key figure in the early London blues-rock scene. The trio of Jagger, Richard and Jones became roommates and musical collaborators. By now, Jagger and Richard had infiltrated Korner's inner circle, sitting in with Blues Incorporated at the Marquee Club. In July 1962, when Korner skipped one of his regular Marquee gigs to appear on a BBC radio show, the three seized the opportunity to debut their own group. The earliest version of the Rolling Stones, featured Jagger, Richard and Jones, plus bassist Dick Taylor, drummer Mick Avory, who was to join the Kinks, and keyboardist Ian Stewart.

Owing to that night's success the Rolling Stones won an eight-month residency at the Crawdaddy Club, where they soon attracted a large fan base. By that time, the group's final line-up had been set, with founding members Jagger, Richards and Jones plus drummer Charlie Watts, another Blues Incorporated member, and bassist Bill Wyman. They also took on a young manager-producer, Andrew Loog Oldham who saw the Stones, the darker, scruffier and more boldly sexual side of rock 'n' roll, as a counterpoint to the Beatles' sunnier, more pop-oriented appearance.

The Rolling Stones first record was 'Come On'/'I Wanna Be Loved', in 1963 for the Decca label. The group's second single, 'I Wanna Be Your Man', was given to them by Lennon and McCartney, thereby establishing from the outset that no real rivalry existed between the Beatles and the Stones. The first half of 1964 saw the Rolling Stones headline their first British tour with the Ronettes and release the single 'Not Fade Away', along with their first album. The Rolling Stones' commercial breakthrough came in mid-1964 with their country-blues version of Bobby Womack's 'It's All Over Now', which went to No 3 in the British charts and just missed the US Top 40. In 1965 the Stones discovered their unique style with the Jagger/Richard-penned singles 'The Last Time' and 'Satisfaction'.

The latter, built around a compelling fuzztone guitar riff from Richard, is more than a standard; many consider it the greatest rock 'n' roll song ever recorded. It captured perfectly the Stones' onstage attitude: rude, raunchy and rebellious. This attitude brought them into conflict with the Establishment, making the group more appealing to their generation who had themselves become disenchanted with the hypocrisies of the adult world. This would solidify into an increasingly militant counter-culture as the decade wore on.

Above: Wyman, Jones, Watts, Jagger and Richard – rude, raunchy and rebellious.

Aftermath, released in April 1966, was the first Stones' album to consist entirely of Jagger-Richard originals. They set aside their blues roots to explore hard rock 'n' roll. The contributions of Brian Jones, the one-time blues purist, were now key to the Stones' eclectic sound, as he coloured the songs with exotic embellishments on a variety of instruments ranging from marimba ('Under My Thumb') to dulcimer ('Lady Jane'). The group's subsequent singles pushed the envelope of outrage, which the Stones were learning to exploit to their benefit. 'Let's Spend the Night Together' was controversial for its title and lyrics.

At mid-decade, the three pre-eminent forces in rock 'n' roll music were the Beatles, Bob Dylan and the Rolling Stones. They influenced one another, and aspects of Dylan's folk-rock and the Beatles' *Rubber Soul* are clearly evident on the Stones' *Between the Buttons*. It remains the group's most understated recording. The Stones then surrendered subtlety for the bombastic psychedelia of *Their Satanic Majesties Request*. It was the band's ironic retort to *Sgt Pepper's Lonely Hearts Club Band*, the Beatles' Summer of Love manifesto.

The year 1967 was an eventful one for the Rolling Stones. Not only did they release three albums, but they were also beset by legal troubles stemming from media-instigated drug busts. When the dust cleared, Jagger, Richard and Jones had narrowly escaped draconian prison sentences. However, whereas the ordeal seemed to strengthen Jagger and Richard's steely resolve, ongoing substance abuse was rapidly causing Jones's physical and mental state to degenerate. He was only marginally involved in sessions for *Beggar's Banquet* and his departure from the group was announced in June 1969, with 'musical differences' being cited as the reason. In July of that

year, Jones was found dead in his swimming pool, the official cause being given as 'death by misadventure'.

Jones's replacement was Mick Taylor, from John Mayall's Bluesbreakers, who made his debut with the Stones at the famous free concert in London's Hyde Park at which Jagger set free thousands of butterflies to fly over London in memory of their friend Brian. The concert attracted 250,000 fans, which was unprecedented at the time, and caused the whole of London to sit up and take notice. The concert launched the Stones' 1969 tour which saw a return to basic rock 'n' roll. The list of Stones classic hits from 1968–69 includes 'Jumping Jack Flash', 'Street Fighting Man', 'Sympathy for the Devil', 'Honky Tonk Women', 'Gimme Shelter' and 'Midnight Rambler'. The last two of these came from their decade-closer *Let It Bleed*, an album filled with portents of violence and social breakdown.

In December 1969 the Rolling Stones staged another free concert – at Altamont Speedway outside San Francisco, barely three months after Woodstock. It symbolically and literally marked the end of the 60s. The Stones, used to the British Hell's Angels providing their security, had no idea that the US Hell's Angels were a rather different breed. Violence ensued, resulting in the stabbing to death of a concert attendee by Hell's Angels. The nightmare of Altamont was forever preserved in the film documentary *Gimme Shelter* and the song 'Sympathy for the Devil'.

In 1971, the Stones launched their own record company, Rolling Stones Records, with the release of *Sticky Fingers* and its raunchy, exuberant first single, 'Brown Sugar'. With a cover designed by Andy Warhol that featured an actual working zipper, its varied musical settings benefited from guitarist Taylor's melodic touch. They followed this fine-tuned work with the masterpiece: the double album *Exile on Main Street*. In 1972 they toured extensively, showcasing this album which helped to refine the parameters of what would become known as 'arena tours'.

The albums kept coming: 'Goat's Head Soup' (1973), 'It's Only Rock 'n' Roll' (1974) and 'Black and Blue' (1976) . Internal factors, including Richard's mounting drug problems, Taylor's abrupt departure in 1974 and Jagger's jet-setting lifestyle, contributed to the air of instability. Ron Wood, a member of the Faces and Rod Stewart's frequent collaborator and accompanist, was chosen as Taylor's replacement for the Stones' 1975 tour and is still a member to this day. Driven by the challenge of the emerging punk-rock scene, the Stones delivered one of the hardest-hitting albums of their career, *Some Girls*, in 1978.

The 1980s yielded the group's best-selling album in the US, *Tattoo You* which stayed at No 1 for nine weeks in 1981. A growing estrangement between Jagger and Richard culminated in a three-year lull after the release of *Dirty Work* (1986). Happily, the stand-off ended when Jagger and Richard successfully resumed their working relationship during a 10-day songwriting retreat in Barbados. The Stones regrouped for an energetic, well-received world tour following the recording of *Steel Wheels*. Preferring to exit on a high note, bassist Wyman retired from the band in 1992. Since the 1990s, all band members have pursued solo careers while also leaving time for Rolling Stones projects. The group is more active now than it has been since the 1970s, releasing studio albums (including the Stones' first Best Rock Album Grammy-winner, *Voodoo Lounge*) and the live *No Security*, and is still doing lengthy world tours and releasing albums. Through it all, no one has yet dethroned the Rolling Stones of their title as the 'greatest rock 'n' roll band in the world'.

Back in mid-60s London, the words on everybody's lips were Carnaby Street. Everyone in London, it seemed, was becoming a 'dedicated follower of fashion'. Another of the bands that found their sound at the Marquee Club was the Kinks.

Above: Sticky Fingers-era Stones: Watts, Taylor, Wyman, Richard and Jagger.

BIOGRAPHY:

The Kinks

In 1963, Londoner Ray Davies joined his younger brother Dave's band, the Ravens, which was soon renamed the Kinks. The original line-up consisted of Ray (guitar, vocals), Dave (lead guitar, vocals), Mick Avory (drums) and Pete Quaife (bass). Today, only the Rolling Stones, which formed in 1962, can claim a lengthier run as an active rock 'n' roll band. Ray Davies is almost indisputably rock's most literate, witty and insightful songwriter. The Kinks' pioneering hard-rock style was evident as far back as 1964 in 'You Really Got Me' which today is considered a forerunner of heavy metal.

They had a number of hits during the mid-1960s, 'You Really Got Me', 'All Day and All of the Night' and 'Tired of Waiting for You' among them. They also wrote satires such as 'A Well Respected Man' and 'Dedicated Follower of Fashion' which was a social commentary that lampooned characters drawn from the heyday of Carnaby Street.

As the popularity of beat-group music faded, Davies' creativity flowered and his songwriting matured. Always a band of anti-trendsetters, the Kinks ignored the counter-culture of the late 1960s in order to reflect on the history of the British Empire.

Their gallery of characters and musical settings was a marriage of understated pop and British music hall, with detours into progressive rock and ethnic music. This was evident on albums such as *Face to Face*, *Something Else* and *Arthur* and in masterpieces such as 'Waterloo Sunset', 'Days', 'Village Green Preservation Society' and 'Sunny Afternoon'.

Though the Kinks struggled commercially and performed unevenly in this period their lack of chart success came to an end with the left-field 'Lola', a song about an encounter with a transvestite. It soon became a staple of their increasingly popular live shows. Ray Davies spent the early 70s composing a series of concept albums (*Preservation*, *Soap Opera* and *Schoolboys in Disgrace*) that were performed as theatrical extravaganzas. Then the group turned its attention to the American market. Their new albums were more popular because of their now hard-hitting sound which resulted in sell-out tours and their first gold albums (*Low Budget*, *One for the Road* and *Give the People What They Want*).

Since then the Kinks, as a band, and brothers Ray and Dave, as solo artists, have continued to produce albums, autobiographies, a BBC film (Ray's *Return to Waterloo* in 1985) and a one-man show.

Since then the Kinks, as a band, and brothers Ray and Dave, as solo artists, have continued to produce albums, autobiographies, a BBC film (Ray's *Return to Waterloo* in 1985) and a one-man show.

The wildest, loudest rock 'n' roll band that London produced at this time was called the Who.

Above: The Kinks, a band of anti-trendsetters.

BIOGRAPHY:

The Who

In 1964 the Who evolved from a group called the High Numbers, which included Roger Daltrey, Pete Townshend and John Entwistle. They were joined by Keith Moon, who'd played in a British surf group called the Beachcombers. The newly charged-up band came on as equipment-smashing Mods who brashly declared, 'Hope I die before I get old', in their stuttering anthem, 'My Generation'. The early Who demonstrated a mastery of the three-minute single, articulating the frustrations of adolescence in such classics as 'Can't Explain', 'Anyway, Anyhow, Anywhere' and 'Substitute'. However, it wasn't until the 1967 release of 'Happy Jack', a piece of art-school whimsy from the album of the same name, that the Who cracked the US Top 40. A turn toward psychedelia and consumerist satire yielded *The Who Sell Out* and its illuminating key song, 'I Can See for Miles'.

Above: The Who – Mod rockers.

In 1969 they released their rock opera *Tommy*, a double-album about the spiritual path of a 'deaf, dumb and blind boy'. An excerpt from *Tommy* provided a concert highlight of the Woodstock festival and its subsequent film documentary. Always one of rock's most hard-hitting live acts, the Who documented this side of their multi-faceted personality with *Live at Leeds* (1970), a record packaged to look like a bootleg. Their next studio recording, *Who's Next*, helped define the sound and sensibility of rock in the 1970s. From the opening track 'Baba O'Riley', a synth-led discourse on 'teenage wasteland' through to Daltrey's electrifying scream on the closing track, 'Won't Get Fooled Again', *Who's Next* stands as a virtual rock primer. From this they returned to the rock-opera format with *Quadrophenia*, a hard-rocking memoir and documentary of the group's Mod origins.

At all stages of their career, the Who have been a dynamic live act. During those decades when they were actively creating, the band were also outspoken and combustible. Group conflicts often fuelled their best work, providing a volatile dynamic that never quite broke them up. In 1978 Keith Moon died of an overdose. The group decided to continue working and recruited a new drummer Kenny Jones (formerly of the Faces) and recorded two more albums, *Face Dances* and *It's Hard*.

The Who undertook a lengthy and much-publicised 'farewell' tour in 1982. Townshend, Daltrey and Entwistle have all pursued prolific solo careers ever since. Among other things, the Who have revived their rock operas *Tommy* and *Quadrophenia* for multi-night stands in big cities and fully fledged concert tours. *Tommy* was also successfully adapted to the Broadway stage in 1993, winning a number of awards. In 1994 they released a box set, *The Who: Thirty Years of Maximum R&B*. The band still regroup on occasion and we 'hope they don't die before they get old'.

The band that was the breeding ground for the top three blues-based guitarists of the 1960s – Eric Clapton, Jeff Beck and Jimmy Page – was the Yardbirds.

BIOGRAPHY:
The Yardbirds

The Yardbirds, who were named after Charlie 'Yardbird' Parker, recorded their early bluesy English hits with Eric Clapton, but he left after recording their first US hit, 'For Your Love' to join John Mayall's Bluesbreakers.

Replacement Jeff Beck was the unassuming lead guitarist for 'Heart Full of Soul', 'Shapes of Things' and 'Over Under Sideways Down'. Original bassist Paul Samwell-Smith quit in summer 1966, and guitarist Chris Dreja switched to bass, leaving room for Jimmy Page, who was present for the recording of the group's last hit, 'Happenings 10 Years' Time Ago' in 1966.

Beck was fired in 1966 for missing shows because of illness. In 1968 drummer Jim McCarty and singer and harmonica player Keith Relf left the band. Jimmy Page formed the New Yardbirds which soon mutated into Led Zeppelin.

BIOGRAPHY:
Eric Clapton

Eric Clapton was born in Surrey in 1945. He started playing guitar at 15 and joined his first group, the Roosters, in early 1963. His first noteworthy band was the Yardbirds, whose 1964 concert recording, *Five Live Yardbirds*, announced Clapton's talent as a fiery blues stylist adept at the group's trademark 'rave-ups'. In 1965 he joined John Mayall's Bluesbreakers and appeared on the remarkable 1966 recording *Bluesbreakers – John Mayall With Eric Clapton*. During his yearlong tenure with Mayall, he earned the nickname 'Slowhand' and inspired the scrawling of 'Clapton Is God' graffiti around London. Next he joined fellow Bluesbreaker Jack Bruce and with Ginger Baker formed 'Cream'. The trio were renowned for their lengthy blues improvisations and arty, blues-based psychedelic pop such as 'White Room'.

Above: Eric 'Clapton is God'.

A January 1973 comeback concert at London's Rainbow Theatre re-introduced him to live performances, but his solo career really commenced a year later with *461 Ocean Boulevard*. Recorded in Miami, and influenced by J.J. Cale and Bob Marley, it topped the album charts in 1974. Meanwhile, Clapton's cover of 'I Shot the Sheriff', originally by Bob Marley and the Wailers, helped introduce reggae to a mass audience. Working with a steady band that included guitarist George Terry, Clapton pursued a mellow, song-oriented course that accentuated his husky, laid-back vocals. His 1970s output included *There's One in Every Crowd* (1975) and *No Reason to Cry* (1976) and he again achieved commercial success in 1977 with *Slowhand*, a strong set that included Clapton's cover of J.J. Cale's 'Cocaine' and 'Lay Down Sally'.

Clapton remained a prolific artist throughout the 1980s, releasing a live double album, *Just One Night*, recording two albums, *Behind the Sun* and *August,* with Phil Collins as producer, and launching his own label, Duck Records, in 1983, with *Money and Cigarettes*. In January 1987, he undertook the first of what would become an annual series of multi-night concerts at London's Royal Albert Hall. In 1992, his career received a major boost from his appearance on MTV's *Unplugged* series. Returning to his blues roots, Clapton next recorded a long-anticipated blues album, *From the Cradle* (1994). Throughout the 90s, he continued to amass hits including 'Tears in Heaven', an elegy for his late son Conor; 'Change the World', a drum-machine collaboration with R&B artist/producer Babyface, which won a Grammy for Record of the Year; and 'My Father's Eyes', a ballad from his 1998 album *Pilgrim*. His unique guitar sound will never be forgotten.

After Cream came a brief alliance with American roots-rockers Delaney and Bonnie, leading to Clapton's first solo album, *Eric Clapton*. 'Betcha didn't think I knew how to rock 'n' roll', he sang in 'Blues Power'. Clapton then formed Derek and the Dominos drawing on the pool of musicians who played on *Eric Clapton*: keyboardist Bobby Whitlock, bassist Carl Radle and drummer Jim Gordon. The double album *Layla ... and Other Assorted Love Songs* (1970) became one of the seminal rock albums of the 1970s, dedicated to Patti Boyd, the then wife of George Harrison. Clapton became addicted to heroin during this period, and a second Derek and the Dominos album was begun but never completed as he became a recluse.

When it comes to guitars, one man alone changed all our concepts of what could be achieved with six strings and a piece of wood – and his name was Jimi Hendrix.

BIOGRAPHY:

Jimi Hendrix

Johnny Allen Hendrix was born in Seattle in 1942, but his name was changed four years later to James Marshall Hendrix. He acquired his first guitar at age 16 and at 17 joined a band, the Rocking Kings. After a short time as a paratrooper, he went on tour with a number of club bands and as a back-up musician for such rhythm and blues artists as Little Richard, the Isley Brothers, Sam Cooke, Jackie Wilson and the Impressions. In 1966 he was discovered by Chas Chandler, the former Animals bassist, while performing in New York with his band, Jimmy James and the Blue Flames. Chandler became Hendrix's manager and brought him to England, where Hendrix became involved in the psychedelic movement, changed his name to 'Jimi' and formed a trio with bassist Noel Redding and drummer Mitch Mitchell.

The Jimi Hendrix Experience recorded three landmark albums – *Are You Experienced?*, *Axis: Bold As Love* and *Electric Ladyland* – in a year and a half. Hendrix's theatrical, incendiary performances at the Monterey Pop and Woodstock festivals, including the ceremonial torching of his guitar at Monterey, have become rock 'n' roll legend.

Under extreme pressure, due to a combination of an arduous touring schedule, sudden fame and drug-taking, the trio broke up in early 1969. Hendrix commenced work on a projected double album and debuted a new group, Band of Gypsies, at the Fillmore East on New Year's Eve 1969. He performed his last concert at the Isle of Fehmarn, Germany, on 6 September 1970 (though he joined Eric Burdon and War on stage on 16 September at Ronnie Scott's in London). On 18 September he died from suffocation, having inhaled vomit as a result of barbiturate intoxication.

In the wake of Hendrix's death, a flood of posthumous albums – everything from old jams from his days as an R&B journeyman to live recordings from his 1967–1970 prime, to previously unreleased or unfinished studio work – were issued. *Voodoo Soup* (1995) was an attempt to reconstruct *First Ray of the New Rising Sun* – the album Hendrix was working on at the time of his death – from tapes, notes, interviews and song lists. He will best be remembered as the man who successfully captured the moods and emotions of the Vietnam generation through his rendition of 'Star Spangled Banner' onstage at Woodstock.

Above: Jimi Hendrix.

Above: Phil Spector created 'The Wall of Sound'.

'LITTLE SYMPHONIES FOR THE KIDDIES' – ROCK 'N' ROLL IN THE EARLY 1960S IN THE USA

Before the British invaded America with the Mersey Sound in the early 1960s, the US music scene was dominated by a musical genius by the name of Phil Spector who is among the greatest producers of rock 'n' roll, and some would passionately argue that he is the greatest ever.

BIOGRAPHY:

Phil Spector

Phil Spector was born Harvey Phillip Spector in the Bronx in 1940. At high school he learnt guitar and piano and began writing and recording original songs with classmate Marshall Lieb. Joined by a third friend, Annette Bard, they formed the Teddy Bears and had a Top 10 hit with 'To Know Him Is to Love Him'. He then co-wrote the classic 'Spanish Harlem' with Jerry Leiber, a big soul hit for Ben E. King. In the early 1960s, he produced hits for such artists as Gene Pitney ('Every Breath I Take'), Curtis Lee ('Pretty Little Angel Eyes') and the Paris Sisters ('I Love How You Love Me'). In 1961, he co-founded the Philles label with

partner Lester Sill, and had an instant hit with 'There's No Other (Like My Baby)', by the Crystals. His ambitious approach to the art of record production helped redefine and revitalise rock 'n' roll during its early-60s slump. On a string of classic records released between 1961 and 1966 on Philles, he elevated the monaural 45 rpm single to an art form. He was totally unique in the way he used the studio and with over-dubbing and orchestral productions he created what became known as 'The Wall of Sound'. The chief ingredient in the Wall of Sound was a cavernous roar created by the fusing of many individual instruments played at maximum volume through an echo chamber.

Spector also had a knack for matching talented singers with expert session musicians and wonderful songs. He worked his charges through endless takes as he tried to materialise the sound he heard in his head. Some of the hits that stand as a testament to his genius include 'Da Doo Ron Ron', 'He's a Rebel' and 'Then He Kissed Me' (by the Crystals); 'Be My Baby', 'Baby, I Love You' and 'Walking in the Rain' (by the Ronettes); 'You've Lost That Lovin' Feelin'', 'Unchained Melody' and 'Ebb Tide' (by the Righteous Brothers); and 'River Deep – Mountain High' (by Ike and Tina Turner).

After the glory days of Top 40 radio began waning in the late 60s, he went on to produce the Beatles' *Let It Be*, John Lennon and Yoko Ono's *Plastic Ono Band* and George Harrison's *All Things Must Pass*, as well as Cher and the Ramones. His production techniques continue to inspire musicians to this day.

Apart from the musicians, the record companies and the producers, rock 'n' roll would not exist without its songwriters and arrangers. Among the foremost of these were Gerry Goffin and Carole King.

BIOGRAPHY:

Goffin & King

Gerry Goffin and Carole King met while attending Queens College, New York, in 1958 and spent evenings together writing songs. After leaving college they married and were immediately hired by Don Kirshner to write songs for his song publishing firm, Aldon Music. King composed music on piano and Goffin wrote the lyrics. They composed hits like a production line from a small cubicle in the Brill Building in New York. Their success was so enormous that Kirshner set up a new label, Dimension, as a special vehicle for them, and they began to produce and arrange their songs as well. They managed to keep abreast of stylistic changes on the vibrant 60s scene, writing with vividness and versatility for British Invasion groups and R&B artists alike. They were also paid a high compliment by the Beatles, who recorded their song 'Chains' and cited Goffin-King as song-writing influences.

Gerry Goffin and Carole King composed a string of timeless hits and classic album tracks for a variety of artists during the 60s, including 'Up On the Roof' (the Drifters), 'One Fine Day' (the Chiffons), 'I'm Into Something Good' (Herman's Hermits), 'Will You Love Me Tomorrow' (the Shirelles), 'Take Good Care of My Baby' (Bobby Vee), 'Chains' (the Cookies), 'Don't Bring Me Down' (the Animals), 'Take a Giant Step' (the Monkees) and 'Goin' Back' (the Byrds). They even used their babysitter to sing one of the songs they'd written and the result, 'The Loco-motion' was a No 1 hit for Little Eva and started a new dance craze.

In 1968, Goffin and King divorced and went their own ways. Goffin continued to write for and with others, while King evolved into a masterful interpreter of her own songs. She became one of the most popular singer/songwriters of the 70s with the release of her album *Tapestry*, which contained such mellow classics as 'It's Too Late' and 'You've Got a Friend'. *Tapestry* was No 1 on the album charts for 15 weeks, earning King a Grammy for Album of the Year in 1971. She followed up with a dozen more albums that kept her star in the ascendant during a magical decade whose extreme moods she helped capture in words and music.

One of the groups that Phil Spector inspired was the Four Seasons.

Above: Gerry Goffin and Carole King churned out hits from the Brill Building in New York.

BIOGRAPHY:

The Four Seasons

As a teenager living in Newark, New Jersey, Frankie Valli sang with the Varietones, who later changed their name to the Four Lovers and had a minor hit in 1956 with 'You're the Apple of My Eye'. With the addition of Bob Gaudio, they changed their name to the Four Seasons and began working with Philadelphia producer Bob Crewe. In addition to Gaudio and Valli, the Four Seasons' line-up included singer/guitarist Tommy DeVito and bass vocalist/vocal arranger Nick Massi. At their peak, they made records that expressed the tough-but-tender emotions of their home turf in the north-east in the same way that the Beach Boys captured the moods of Southern California in their songs.

The Four Seasons and the Beach Boys were virtually the only American groups whose successful careers were not affected when the Beatles and the British Invasion bands arrived in the USA in 1964. In fact, that year ranked as the Four Seasons' most successful,

despite the competition from the UK. This was because of the Four Seasons' ability to complement Italian-American doo-wop harmonies with the powerful falsetto and three-octave range of lead vocalist Frankie Valli, flawless song-writing from group member Bob Gaudio, and arrangements and production that drew upon everything from Phil Spector's 'Wall of Sound' to the dance beat of Motown's style. During their hit-making years of 1962–68, the Four Seasons had over 20 Top 40 singles, including No 1s 'Sherry', 'Big Girls Don't Cry', 'Walk Like a Man' and 'Rag Doll'.

In 1975, a re-formed Four Seasons built around Valli and Gaudio hit the top of the charts again with 'Who Loves You' and 'December, 1963 (Oh, What a Night)'. Valli has since enjoyed success as a solo artist with 'My Eyes Adored You' and 'Grease', both of which went to No 1 in the USA. They have sold over 100 million records, making them the most successful white vocal group in rock 'n' roll history.

Above: The Four Seasons – the most successful white vocal group in rock 'n' roll history.

'IT'S ALL OVER NOW, BABY BLUE' – FOLK ROCK

The modern American folk movement dates back to the strong unionisation movement of the 1930s. Then during the war years the folksingers Leadbelly and Woody Guthrie reinforced the movement's values in their songs and performances. It flowered in the early 1950s with the folk songs of the Weavers, but the McCarthy era with its 'witchhunts' drove protest music underground.

Throughout the 1950s the creators and audiences of pop music seemed only interested in trivialities expressed in lyrics of unrequited love, agonised courtship, narcissistic fulfilment and suicidal loss alongside novelty songs and abstract instrumentals. Nevertheless, there were writers and singers who presented unorthodox situations in their songs by expressing attitudes of defiance, rejection and resistance which were not simply the petulant outbursts of adolescents.

Songs of protest against the status quo began to emerge again in the early stages of the Vietnam War. One man's career reflects these developments like a mirror.

Bob Dylan was the pre-eminent poet/lyricist and songwriter of his time. He re-energised the folk-music genre, bringing a new lyrical depth to rock 'n' roll when he went electric, and bridged the worlds of rock and country music. His songs have provided a running commentary on an ever-changing age. His biting, and often cryptic lyrics captured and defined the mood of a generation.

Above: Woody Guthrie, Bob Dylan's mentor.

BIOGRAPHY:

Bob Dylan

Bob Dylan was born Robert Zimmerman in 1941, in Duluth, Minnesota. He learned to play harmonica and piano by the age of 10 and was a self-taught guitarist. At high-school in the late 1950s, he listened to Hank Williams and Little Richard and learned how to play rock 'n' roll. While attending the University of Minnesota, Dylan traded his electric guitar for an acoustic and began to copy folk-singers of the previous generation, including his mentor Woody Guthrie. In December 1960, Dylan moved to New York City, where he gravitated to the folk and blues scene in Greenwich Village. His New York City debut occurred at Gerdes' Folk City on 11 April 1961, with Dylan opening for John Lee Hooker. After playing harmonica on a session for folk-singer Carolyn Hester, Dylan was signed by producer John Hammond to Columbia Records.

On his first album he recorded topical folk songs, accompanying himself on harmonica and guitar. The album contained only two originals ('Song for Woody' and 'Talking New York'). In May 1963 he released the almost entirely self-composed *The Freewheelin' Bob Dylan* which included classics such as 'Blowin' in the Wind', 'Masters of War' and 'A Hard Rain's A-Gonna Fall'. These songs astonished the intelligentsia in folk circles and established Dylan as a formidable composer. In early 1964, as the Beatles began conquering the youth of America, the articulate and challenging Dylan occupied the minds of a slightly older set. He released two albums that year: the politically cynical *The Times They Are a-Changin'* and *Another Side of Bob Dylan*, which represented the artist in a more introspective mood with songs such as 'My Back Pages' and 'It Ain't Me, Babe'.

Dylan's gradual move from folk to rock 'n' roll was inspired by the Beatles and the Byrds, whose electrified folk-rock arrangement of Dylan's 'M. Tambourine Man' eventually went to No 1 in June 1965. He then released *Bringing It All Back Home*, one side of which was acoustic and the other electric. His lyrics were as literate and demanding as ever, but on songs like 'Subterranean Homesick Blues' they were now set to rock 'n' roll. In May 1965 Dylan undertook his first tour of the UK. That stormy affair was documented in stark black and white by filmmaker D.A. Pennebaker in *Don't Look Back*. Dylan returned to the States and in July 1965 strode onstage at the Newport Festival with an electric guitar in hand and the Paul Butterfield Blues Band backing him up. He was booed offstage after only three songs, at which point he returned with an acoustic guitar and a strong message for all the folk purists: 'It's All Over Now, Baby Blue'.

A few weeks later, Dylan had his first major hit with 'Like a Rolling Stone', a scornful six-minute epistle which was the opening track on *Highway 61 Revisited*, a landmark pop album that set Dylan's surrealistic verse to raw and hot rock 'n' roll. In early 1966 he headed to Nashville to record the double album *Blonde on Blonde*, which was a career milestone Recorded with the cream of country-music session musicians, it included the hit singles 'Rainy Day Women No 12 & 35' and 'I Want You', as well as deeper pieces such as 'Just Like a Woman', 'Visions of Johanna' and the side-long 'Sad-Eyed Lady of the Lowlands'. That spring, he embarked on a stormy world tour that found him backed by the Hawks (later known as the Band) and

Above: Bob Dylan captured and defined the mood of a generation.

confronting audiences that still hadn't forgiven him for going electric. On 29 July he was seriously injured in a motorcycle accident near his home in Woodstock, New York. Dylan dropped out of sight for a year and a half, rehearsing and recording with the Band at their home studio. These sessions were repeatedly bootlegged and finally saw legitimate release in 1975 as *The Basement Tapes*.

His next release was *John Wesley Harding*, a folk-country album of inscrutable parables about historical characters. Jimi Hendrix took one of its songs, 'All Along the Watchtower', and turned it into an electrified, apocalyptic anthem of the age. Dylan changed course again in December 1969 with his most overtly 'country' record, *Nashville Skyline*, singing lightweight songs like 'Lay Lady Lay' in a newly mellowed voice.

While Dylan was the uncontested voice and conscience of the 60s, his presence seemed somewhat less powerful in the following decades, especially on such lesser works as *Self-Portrait* and *Street-Legal*, as well as on a number of live albums. All the same, he excelled himself on recordings such as 1975's *Blood On the Tracks*. After forming the Rolling Thunder Revue with an inspired bunch of troubadours, he took it out on the road. In 1976, Dylan released another excellent record, *Desire*, and provided some of the most riveting performances at the Band's farewell concert, *The Last Waltz*.

Beginning in 1979, Dylan took another of his unexpected career turns by promoting Christianity on a trio of albums (*Slow Train Coming*, *Saved*, *Shot of Love*). Thereafter, he resumed his more generally secular but no less moralistic commentary on such albums as *Infidels* (1983), *Empire Burlesque* (1985) and *Oh Mercy* (1989).

Dylan's next album of original material, *Under the Red Sky*, appeared in 1991. Since then, he has recorded two albums of unadorned folk songs and spent the rest of his time on the road like the wandering minstrel that he really is. The musicians that Bob Dylan spent most of the 1960s with eventually became a group in their own right, simply called the Band who, more than any other group, put rock 'n' roll back in touch with its roots. They projected a sense of community in the turbulent late 1960s and early 1970s – a time when the fabric of community in the United States was fraying.

Above: The Basement Tapes – the bootlegged sessions with the Band.

BIOGRAPHY:

The Band

They began as the Hawks. Four of the band – guitarist Robbie Robertson, bassist Rick Danko, organist Garth Hudson and pianist Richard Manuel – were from Canada; the drummer, Levon Helm, was from Arkansas. The Hawks toured the States until late 1963, at which point the backing musicians split from their vocalist Ronnie Hawkins to continue on their own as Levon and the Hawks.

Guitarist Robertson drew from history in his evocative, cinematic story-songs. Bassist Rick Danko, drummer Levon Helm and keyboardist Richard Manuel provided the rustic harmonies with multi-instrumentalist Garth Hudson filling in an atmosphere of country rock 'n' roll.

Bob Dylan recruited them as his back-up group for a 1965–66 world tour. As the Hawks, without their drummer, they helped effect Dylan's transformation from an acoustic folk singer to an electric rock 'n' roller. The shows were revelatory and controversial; when Dylan and the Hawks plugged in and played with electrifying abandon, they aroused horror amongst the folk traditionalists. One of the most legendary of all his rock concerts was in Manchester when Dylan, backed by Robertson, Manuel, Danko, Hudson and drummer Mickey Jones, faced down a hostile audience. This finally saw official release in 1998 as *Bob Dylan Live 1966*.

Dylan's collaboration with the former Hawks continued throughout 1966. Working with Dylan at a rented house in Woodstock, they created a body of material that would eventually see release as *The Basement Tapes*. At the same time, now calling themselves the Band, they recorded a large number of their own original songs which were released as *Music from Big Pink* and on side four of Dylan's *Basement Tapes*. Most of the songs were written by guitarist Robbie Robertson, including his masterpiece 'The Weight', which was steeped in Biblical imagery. Dylan collaborated on 'Tears of Rage' with Manuel and 'This Wheel's on Fire' with Danko. His hymn-like 'I Shall Be Released', closed the album. *Music from Big Pink* was one of the most influential albums of the 60s, heralding the arrival of a more roots-oriented movement in rock 'n' roll.

In 1969 they released an album simply called *The Band*, regarded as their signature work. This drew on the strengths of Robertson's song-writing ('Up On Cripple Creek', 'The Night They Drove Old Dixie Down'), and the band members' empathetic musicianship, with the harmonising voices of Helm, Danko and Manuel.

More albums followed – *Stage Fright* in 1970 and then *Cahoots* in 1971. The Band performed at Woodstock, the Isle of Wight and Watkins Glen, and they maintained a gruelling schedule as a touring band. On 31 December 1971, they performed a New Year's Eve concert that marked their last performance for one and a half years.

In 1973 the Band recorded an album of oldies called *Moondog Matinee* (a reference to Alan Freed) and reunited with Dylan for the *Planet Waves* album and tour which resulted in the live album *Before the Flood*. They recorded the best of their later albums in 1975 *Northern Lights, Southern Cross* and then took their leave in 1976 with a memorable final concert *The Last Waltz* held at San Francisco's Winterland Ballroom.

They were joined onstage by legends such as Muddy Waters, Bob Dylan, Van Morrison, Neil Young, Eric Clapton and Joni Mitchell. The show was recorded and released as a film and triple-album set.

Since then, Robertson has composed film soundtracks and directed his own project, *Carny* as well as having a solo career that began with 1987's *Robbie Robertson*. Levon Helm went into acting as well as recording six solo albums. Rick Danko was the first member of the Band to release a solo record – 1977's *Rick Danko* – and worked with Eric Andersen and Norwegian singer/songwriter Jonas Fjeld.

The original band members, minus Robertson, regrouped and began touring in 1983. Three years later, their troubled pianist, Richard Manuel, hanged himself in a Florida motel room after a club performance. The surviving members continued as the Band and released *Jericho*, their first album of new music in 16 years. Danko died in December 1999.

Like the Band the Byrds built their sound upon three-part harmonies.

BIOGRAPHY:

The Byrds

Before the Byrds formed in 1964 Roger McGuinn had been a folk-music accompanist for such acts as the Limelighters, the Chad Mitchell Trio and Judy Collins. Singer/guitarists David Crosby and Gene Clark were West Coast folkies, while bassist Chris Hillman and drummer Michael Clarke had bluegrass and rock backgrounds, respectively. Vocal harmonies were a feature of the LA pop scene, which also boasted the Beach Boys, Jan and Dean, the Mamas and the Papas, and the Turtles McGuinn's 12-string playing bore elements of both John Coltrane's modal jazz innovations and the drone of an Indian raga. This sense of mystery informed the Byrds' best work, from their groundbreaking remake of Dylan's 'Mr Tambourine Man' to their classic send-up of the celebrity life, 'So You Want to Be a Rock 'n' Roll Star'.

By the time the Byrds recorded their *Sweetheart of the Rodeo* album in 1968, original members Clark and Crosby had dropped out and country-rock pioneer Gram Parsons had joined for a brief but influential stay. McGuinn was the only original member of the four-man line-up that lasted from 1969 to 72, which included guitarist Clarence White, bassist Skip Battin and drummer Gene Parsons. This version of the Byrds

recorded several albums, including the double album *Untitled*, and evolved into a tightly knit performing band. The five original Byrds convened for a reunion album in 1973, but by this time the group members were all successfully pursuing separate careers: McGuinn and Clark as solo artists; Crosby as part of the harmony-based supergroup Crosby, Stills and Nash; Hillman as a solo artist but subsequently finding success in the country-music field with the Desert Rose Band; and Clarke as drummer for Firefall.

Gene Clark died in 1991 and Michael Clarke died in 1993. McGuinn, Hillman and Crosby reunited to perform as the Byrds in 1989, in order to reclaim the name legally, and recorded four songs for the *Byrds* box set, released in 1990. During their peak years of 1965–1967, the Byrds were in the US Top 40, seven times.

Above: The Byrds built their sound upon three-part harmonies.

FREAK OUT – WEST COAST ROCK

The West Coast of America has always been synonymous with decadence and excess but during the late 1960s it became progressively more so. Drugs have also been synonymous with popular music and in the late 1960s on the West Coast a new drug entered the music scene. The fans were encouraged to 'turn on, tune in, drop out' – which they did in their thousands. The drug was called LSD, supposedly celebrated by the Beatles themselves in their song 'Lucy in the Sky with Diamonds'.

Suddenly thousands of young, hip American teenagers arrived in San Francisco to celebrate their own liberation from perceived parental and government control and a new culture was born. They called themselves 'Hippies' or sometimes 'Freaks'. The culture was driven by the drug-inspired West Coast music, and rock 'n' roll moved away from its original African roots to a more melodic and abstract form.

This change had been developing on the West Coast for a number of years. Its earliest form was epitomised by the Pacific coast surfing community and their band was called the Beach Boys.

BIOGRAPHY:
The Beach Boys

The Beach Boys consisted of three brothers, Brian, Dennis and Carl Wilson, their cousin Mike Love, and a friend, Alan Jardine, who all grew up in the Los Angeles suburb of Hawthorne. Brian Wilson, who demonstrated an aptitude for music at an early age, was the group's leader, orchestrating their harmonies, writing the music and producing the recording sessions. One of the few undisputed geniuses in popular music, Brian possessed an uncanny gift for harmonic invention and complex vocal and instrumental arrangements. Initially, the magnitude of that genius was overlooked owing to the subject matter of the band's early hits, surfing, hot rods, girls etc. But even the lyrics are celebrated today for their deft use of technical lingo, on the one hand, and youthful naivety, on the other.

The Beach Boys' earliest hits – 'Surfin'', 'Surfin' Safari', 'Surfin' USA', and 'Surfer Girl', all released in 1962–63 – helped raise the profile of the state of California and the sport of surfing. The group also celebrated the Golden State's obsession with hot-rod racing ('Shut Down', '409', 'Little Deuce Coupe') and the pursuit of happiness by carefree high-schoolers in less complicated times ('Be True to Your School', 'Fun, Fun, Fun', 'I Get Around'). The Beach Boys' first golden era lasted from 1962 to 65, when they charted 16 hit singles in a very competitive Top 40.

The increasing sophistication of the Beach Boys' arrangements around this time was due to the fact that Brian quit touring with the band in December 1964 in order to work full-time on their recordings back home in California. His maturation resulted in such harmony-filled pop opuses as 'Help me, Rhonda'

and 'California Girls', as well as the increasingly adventurous tracks to be found on such albums as 1965's *The Beach Boys Today!* While the Beach Boys were off touring with their growing treasure chest of hit singles, Brian began work in January 1966 on *Pet Sounds*. He laboured over it non-stop for four months, enlisting an orchestra of session musicians to help him chase the 'pet sounds' he heard in his head. At the end, the Beach Boys returned to add their voices to the finished instrumental tracks. *Pet Sounds* sold disappointingly as an album, though it yielded a bounty of singles, including 'Wouldn't It Be Nice', 'God Only Knows' and 'Sloop John B'.

Above: The Beach Boys – America's band.

Brian pressed on to his next project, 'Good Vibrations', which packed an album's worth of ideas and production tricks into one song. 'Good Vibrations' returned the Beach Boys to the top of the charts and added a new phrase to street slang. Thereafter, Brian threw himself into an even more ambitious album project, *Smile*, that wound up collapsing under the weight of Wilson's fragile psyche and increasingly erratic behaviour, at least in part triggered by his experimentation with drugs. *Smile* was never finished; in its place came a diluted facsimile, *Smiley Smile*.

The Beach Boys reacted by bonding into a more closely knit, democratic unit and recording a series of low-key albums, including *Friends* and *Wild Honey*. In 1970 they moved from Capitol to Reprise Records and released one of their strongest group efforts, *Sunflower*, which spotlighted the individual talents of all three Wilson brothers (especially the suddenly prolific Dennis). During the 70s, the Beach Boys became an in-demand touring act whose popularity soared as the rock audience rediscovered all the old hits, which had come and gone so quickly in the previous decade. Capitol Records' release of *Endless Summer*, a double-LP greatest-hits collection, surprisingly streaked to the top of the album charts, and the Beach Boys were suddenly hot all over again. Touted as 'America's band', they also benefited from all the media attention surrounding the rescue and recovery of their leader Brian from a series of lost years spent in drug-induced exile. With the

"Brian's back' publicity campaign of 1976 came *15 Big Ones*, their first new album in three and a half years, and a renascent creative momentum. It was followed in 1977 by *The Beach Boys Love You*, which displayed more of Brian's involvement than any album since *Pet Sounds* and remains a cult favourite among Beach Boys aficionados.

Subsequently, the band intermittently released new albums and toured like clockwork every summer while making headlines for various extracurricular mishaps: the accidental death by drowning of Dennis Wilson in 1983 and the legal battles between band members including Mike Love's lawsuit against Brian Wilson, wherein he claimed to have co-authored certain Beach Boys songs credited to Brian alone. At times the Beach Boys have seemed to be rock 'n' roll's longest-running soap opera. Yet they have been responsible for some of the most perfect harmonies and gorgeous melodies in rock 'n' roll history, and it is for this vast accumulation of timeless music that they will ultimately be remembered and celebrated. Carl Wilson died of cancer in 1998.

Early hippie music was mostly experimental as the musicians were taking hallucinogenic drugs at the same time as attempting to create music. Sometimes the result was chaotic and at other times sublime. Eventually record companies recognised that it had commercial viability and began signing up hippie bands, most of whom would drop by the wayside because they were too stoned to deliver. However, one of the first bands to be signed was not only to have world-wide commercial success but would create a new style of rock 'n' roll for the consumer. This new style was poetic, spiritual and sexual all at the same time. The genius who fronted this band was called Jim Morrison and the band was called the Doors.

BIOGRAPHY:

The Doors

The Doors formed in the summer of 1965 around Jim Morrison and Ray Manzarek, who had met at UCLA's film school. A year later the group signed with Elektra Records, recording six landmark studio LPs and a live album for the label. They achieved popular success and critical acclaim for all their albums including their 1967 debut, *The Doors* (which included their 11-minute epic 'The End' and 'Light My Fire', a No 1 hit at the height of the Summer of Love). As their career wore on, however, Morrison's problems with drugs and alcohol resulted in increasingly erratic behaviour, culminating in an alleged incident of exposure onstage at a March 1969 concert in Miami.

The Doors rebounded from this adversity with one of their finest albums, *LA Woman*, which contained the Top 40 hits 'Love Her Madly' and 'Riders On the Storm'. After its release, Morrison took leave of absence from the Doors and moved to Paris, where he allegedly died of a heart attack on 3 July 1971.

In 1991 Oliver Stone released a film entitled *The Doors*, starring Val Kilmer as the legendary Jim Morrison. It controversially portrayed Morrison as the shamanic figure he believed himself to be.

One of Morrison's girlfriends also had considerable success and a tragic ending. Her name was Janis Joplin.

Above: Jim Morrison and the Doors.

BIOGRAPHY:

Janis Joplin

Janis Joplin, nicknamed 'Pearl', was born in 1943 in Port Arthur, Texas. Growing up, she was a social outcast who found an outlet in music. Joplin was drawn to blues (Odetta, Leadbelly and Bessie Smith) and soul (Otis Redding, Tina Turner and Etta James). She performed folk-blues on the coffee-house circuit in Texas and San Francisco before hooking up with Big Brother and the Holding Company – guitarists James Gurley and Sam Andrew, bassist Peter Albin and drummer David Getz – at the suggestion of Chet Helms, a hip entrepreneur and fellow Texan.

Big Brother were loud, explosive and deliberately crude in their blend of blues and psychedelia. Helms, one of a group of event organisers who called themselves the Family Dog, booked the group on some of the earliest bills on the emerging San Francisco scene where they became regulars. *Cheap Thrills* was an explosive showcase of psychedelic soul featuring Joplin's raw, impassioned readings of Willie Mae Thornton's 'Ball and Chain' and 'Piece of My Heart'. The latter song had originally been recorded by Erma Franklin, the younger sister of Aretha, and was written by Jerry Ragavoy who also wrote 'Cry Baby', 'Get It While You Can' and 'Try (Just a Little Bit Harder)'. He was Joplin's favourite songwriter.

Joplin left Big Brother in December 1968, releasing her first solo album, *I've Got Dem Ol' Kozmic Blues Again Mama!*, in 1969, and she toured extensively with her Kozmic Blues Band. By mid-1970, however, she had formed a new band called Full-Tilt Boogie. They toured for several months and entered the studio to record what would turn out to be Joplin's swan song.

Joplin had often sought refuge in drugs and alcohol, and she was found dead of a heroin overdose in a Hollywood hotel room in October 1970. The posthumously released *Pearl* consisted of nine finished tracks and one instrumental to which she was supposed to have added vocals on the day she died. It was prophetically titled 'Buried Alive in the Blues'.

Pearl became Joplin's biggest seller and included 'Me and Bobby McGee', a song written for her by Kris Kristofferson, her ex-lover. A tender portrait of a counter-cultural love affair, sung by Joplin as a road-weary country blues, 'Me and Bobby McGee' perfectly captured the bohemian spirit of the times.

The psychedelic movement of West Coast America was hugely promoted by Bill Graham, who encouraged and supported many of the bands through a series of open-air festivals and concerts at his dance halls, the most famous being the Fillmore in San Francisco. One of the bands that epitomises this drug-fuelled culture was called the Grateful Dead.

Above: Janis Joplin — a social outcast who found an outlet in music.

The Grateful Dead

Initially known as Mother McCree's Uptown Jug Champions and later the Warlocks, they provided musical settings for novelist and cult leader Ken Kesey's fabled Acid Tests. After settling on the name the Grateful Dead, they began honing their concert alchemy at San Francisco's psychedelic ballrooms. The Dead fused rock 'n' roll energy with the psychedelic experience to fashion an endlessly elaborate interplay of sound. The keyboardist position was the most unstable in the band, as no fewer than three of the Dead's keyboard players died during their 30-year history, resonating with fate of the drummers in the spoof movie *Spinal Tap*.

Highlights of the group's recorded legacy include *Anthem of the Sun* (1968), their ultra-psychedelic *Live/Dead* (1969), a concert compendium that bore out fans' claims that the Dead were best experienced in concert, *Workingman's Dead* and *American Beauty* (both from 1970), country- and folk-influenced classics that highlighted their song-writing ability and sage-like overview of the West Coast counter-culture, and *Grateful Dead* (a.k.a. *Skull and Roses*), another multi-album live set. The mystical band-fan bonding ritual drove the music to improvisational peaks. Led by Jerry Garcia's modal guitar work, and taking cues from sources as varied as Jimmy Reed, John Coltrane and Bill Monroe, the Dead would delve into blues, folk, jazz, R&B and avant-garde realms for hours on end.

During the latter half of their career, Garcia was periodically beset with drug problems, a state of affairs that came to a head with his arrest on drug possession

charges in 1985 and his collapse into a near-fatal diabetic coma in 1986. His health improved in the wake of those crises, revitalising the Dead through a period of heightened activity that included the 1987 hit album *In the Dark* and US Top 40 single 'Touch of Grey'. However, drugs continued to haunt the Grateful Dead, who lost keyboardist Brent Mydland to a fatal overdose in 1990. Garcia himself died on 9 August 1995, at a treatment facility in Forest Knolls, California, where he'd gone to seek help for his heroin addiction. They played their last concert the previous month at Soldier Field in Chicago.

Another band who regularly played at Bill Graham's Fillmore were called Jefferson Airplane.

Above: The Grateful Dead in their natural habitat.

BIOGRAPHY:

Jefferson Airplane

Marty Balin founded Jefferson Airplane in 1965. Their first album was *Jefferson Airplane Takes Off*. When their first singer left to raise a family, she was replaced by the charismatic Grace Slick who had been a member of the Great Society. Slick brought with her a pair of songs, the psychedelic 'White Rabbit' and the driving 'Somebody to Love', that would become rock classics.

The adventurous Airplane took unprecedented liberties on record and in concert. The band members had eclectic musical influences: Paul Kantner came from a folk background, Jorma Kaukonen was a blues aficionado, Jack Casady grew up playing R&B, and Spencer Dryden boasted jazz training in his background; Balin was a pop crooner and Slick's tastes were literary and offbeat. These various strands, brought together in the heady, experimental cauldron of San Francisco in the mid-60s, made for an electrifying union that changed rock music forever. The five Jefferson Airplane albums released from 1967 to 1969 – *Surrealistic Pillow*, *After Bathing at Baxter's*, *Crown of Creation*, *Bless Its Pointed Little Head* and *Volunteers* were amongst the most exciting and innovative records from the West Coast.

Surrealistic Pillow (1967) yielded the Top 10 hits 'Somebody to Love' and 'White Rabbit', making the Airplane the most commercially successful band on the underground-oriented San Francisco scene. The album stayed on the charts for over a year and peaked at No 3. At the same time *Surrealistic Pillow* included psychedelic raves with titles like '3/5 Mile in Ten Seconds', 'She Has Funny Cars' and 'Plastic Fantastic

Lover'. It closed with a lengthy, improvised and chorus-free ballad, 'Comin' Back to Me', which featured the Grateful Dead's Jerry Garcia on guitar.

Appearing in late 1967, after the bloom had faded from the flower-power Summer of Love, *After Bathing at Baxter's* shows the Airplane at a creative zenith. Its songs were arranged into five 'suites' that ran for up to 12 minutes. The inspired songwriting, most of it by Kantner, captured the utopian credo of San Francisco in the late 60s. The group worked on the album from June to October of 1967, defying record company demands and deadlines. In so doing, they helped trigger a shift in the music industry that placed creative control back into the hands of the musicians.

Crown of Creation, which appeared in 1968, displayed an increasingly political stance and *Bless Its Pointed Little Head* served as their first live recording. In 1969 the Airplane performed at both the Woodstock and Altamont rock festivals and released their most overtly political album, *Volunteers*. Thereafter, the group gradually broke down under the weight of differing musical tastes. Kaukonen and Casady paid increasing attention to their blues-based side project, Hot Tuna, while Kantner premiered the name Jefferson Starship on a 1970 side project entitled *Blows Against the Empire*. In 1971, the still-intact Airplane launched a custom label, Grunt, which released records by the band, its offshoots and friends. Several more Airplane albums followed, including *Bark* (1971) and *Long John Silver* (1972). Their 'best of' album was called *The Worst of Jefferson Airplane*.

One of the psychedelic funsters of this era was a man who, unusually, was not a drug-taker. He was first and foremost a highly talented composer and only used rock 'n' roll as a vehicle so that he could continue composing; the man who believed that 'music is the best' was Frank Zappa.

BIOGRAPHY:
Frank Zappa

Frank Vincent Zappa was born in Baltimore, Maryland, in 1940. He was gifted with a keen interest in chemistry and music from an early age but chose the latter. He became conversant in everything from doo-wop to the classical composition of Bartok and Stravinsky and Edgar Varese, whose dissonant music he loved.

In 1965, Zappa formed the Mothers of Invention (later, simply the Mothers), who were deliberately and mischievously unconventional. From the way they dressed to the music they played, Zappa intended the Mothers to be provocative and controversial. The first album they released, *Freak Out* (1966) contained a deluge of traditional rock n' roll teenage sob songs, doo-wop and R&B played with tongue firmly in cheek.

Zappa brought a high degree of compositional sophistication to a genre that had typically taken its cues from the simplistic chord progressions of songs like 'Louie, Louie' whilst acknowledging the naive genius behind it. Zappa greatly extended the range of rock, composing

oratorios, symphonic pieces, ballets, digitised extravaganzas for the Synclavier keyboard, and satirical musicals. He was a brilliant guitarist, his 'Watermelon in Easter Hay' from the *Joe's Garage* album really showing his talents. Over the years he employed many musicians and pushed them to their musical limits, expanding the boundaries of rock. He died of cancer in December 1993 but left behind one of the largest, most varied and, some would say, strangest catalogues of music and was one of the greatest contributors to the huge changes that rock 'n' roll music underwent during the 1960s and beyond.

During the 1970s, the changes in rock 'n' roll that the 1960s engendered peaked. One of the most significant changes was in the technology that had been developed, firstly, so that the bands could firstly be heard in the large concert e hat were increasingly being use d and, secondly, in the recording techniques t icians themselves were demandin The 1970s saw the rise of the huge extravaganzas that he marriage of rock music and theatre could achieve. It was no longer enough for a band to be talented musicians. They had to be backed up with huge sound systems, vast arrays of flashing lights and glamorous lifestyles.

Above: 'Music is the best' – Frank Zappa.

WE WILL ROCK YOU

GOING TO CALIFORNIA – EARLY 70S ROCK

Combining the visceral power and intensity of hard rock with the finesse and delicacy of British folk music, Led Zeppelin redefined rock in the 1970s and for all time. They were as influential in that decade as the Beatles were in the previous one. Their impact extends to classic and alternative rockers alike. Then and now, Led Zeppelin looms larger than life on the rock landscape as a band for the ages with an almost mystical power to evoke primal passions.

Above: Led Zeppelin – the 'greatest rock band in the world'.

The 1970s

BIOGRAPHY:
Led Zeppelin

In 1968 Jimmy Page formed Led Zeppelin from the ashes of the Yardbirds. Before the Yardbirds (1966–1968), Page was one of Britain's most in-demand session guitarists. He performed on mid-60s records by Donovan ('Hurdy Gurdy Man'), Them ('Gloria'), the Kinks ('You Really Got Me'), the Who ('I Can't Explain') amongst many others. Page assembled a 'New Yardbirds' in order to fulfil contractual obligations which then freed him to form his dream band. Bassist and keyboard player John Paul Jones' resumé also included session work for the Rolling Stones, Donovan, Jeff Beck and Dusty Springfield. Singer Robert Plant and drummer John 'Bonzo' Bonham, both from Birmingham, had previously played in the Band of Joy.

The group's use of familiar blues-rock forms spiced with exotic flavours found favour among the rock audience that emerged in the 1970s. Led Zeppelin aimed at the album market, eschewing the singles orientation of the previous decade. Their self-titled first album found them elongating blues forms with extended solos and psychedelic effects, most notably on the agonised 'Dazed and Confused', and hard-rock rave-ups like 'Good Times Bad Times' and 'Communication Breakdown'.

Led Zeppelin II found them further tightening up and modernising their blues-rock approach on classic tracks such as 'Whole Lotta Love' which was built around Page's heavyweight guitar riffs, Plant's raw, half-screamed vocals, Jones' rock-solid bass patterns and Bonzo's primal drumming (subsequently the tune was used as the theme tune for Top of the Pops for years).

Led Zeppelin III took a more acoustic, folk-oriented approach with songs like 'Gallows Pole' and their own 'Tangerine', yet they also rocked furiously on 'Immigrant Song' and offered a lengthy electric blues with 'Since I've Been Loving You'.

In 1971 they released Led Zeppelin IV, a rock milestone and their defining work. The album was a hybrid of the folk and hard rock they had been pursuing, particularly on 'When the Levee Breaks' and the haunting 'The Battle of Evermore'. 'Black Dog' was a hard-rock number in the same vein as 'Whole Lotta Love'. Most significant of the album's eight tracks was the eight-minute epic 'Stairway to Heaven' that remains radio's all-time most-requested rock song, although never released as a single. Their fifth album, Houses of the Holy, with its startling cover, ws full of adventuresome and humorous music, including such masterpieces as 'The Song Remains the Same' and the Jamaican-styled 'D'yer Mak'er'. Physical Graffiti, a double album, followed in 1975 and included 'In My Time of Dying', 'Ten Years Gone' and the lengthy, middle-Eastern flavoured 'Kashmir'.

Led Zeppelin's sold-out concert tours became rituals of high-energy rock 'n' roll theatre. Their film documentary *The Song Remains the Same* from 1976, attests to the group's powerful appeal at the height of their popularity. The darker side of Led Zeppelin – their reputation as one of the most hedonistic and indulgent of all rock bands– is an undeniable facet of the band's history. They mirror the legend of Robert Johnson meeting the devil at the crossroads through their alleged dabblings with the occult.

In the mid-to-late 70s, a series of tragedies befell Led Zeppelin. Three years passed between the release of *Presence* (1976) and *In Through the Out Door*, their final studio album (1979), and on 25 September 1980 drummer John Bonham was found dead. Knowing he was irreplaceable, Led Zeppelin disbanded.

Led Zeppelin have sold over 85 million units. *Led*

Zeppelin IV is the fourth best-selling album in history, having sold more than 22 million copies, and four other albums by the band – *Physical Graffiti*, *Led Zeppelin II*, *Houses of the Holy* and *Led Zeppelin* – also rank among the all-time top 100 best-sellers. Fittingly, Led Zeppelin are tied with the Beatles (five apiece) for the most albums on that esteemed list – a mark of both bands' impact. If the Beatles can be considered the 'greatest pop group in the world' and the Rolling Stones the 'greatest rock 'n' roll band in the world', then Led Zeppelin are indisputably the 'greatest rock band in the world'.

Led Zeppelin achieved major success first in America. Another band who were largely unrecognised in their own country and found their fame in California were Fleetwood Mac.

BIOGRAPHY:

Fleetwood Mac

Fleetwood Mac began in 1967 when Peter Green, Mick Fleetwood and John McVie, who were all members of John Mayall's Bluesbreakers, decided to form a band of their own. McVie and Fleetwood had been playing with Mayall, a British blues legend, since 1963 and 1965, respectively, while Green replaced Eric Clapton in 1966. Initially a quartet, the original Fleetwood Mac also included guitarist Jeremy Spencer and then expanded with the addition of Danny Kirwan prior to their second album. Not surprisingly, the group's first two albums *Fleetwood Mac* (1967) and *Mr Wonderful* (1967) were heavily blues-oriented. 'Black Magic Woman', a Peter Green song from the latter album, later became a major hit for Santana. In 1969, Fleetwood Mac went to America and recorded at Chicago's Chess studios with blues musicians Willie Dixon and Otis Spann. The result was released as the two-volume *Blues Jam* in the UK and as *Fleetwood Mac in Chicago* in the US. By decade's end, however, Fleetwood Mac had begun moving from traditional blues to more progressive rock.

There are arguably three 'definitive' Fleetwood Mac line-ups. One of them is the blues-oriented band of the late 60s, which arrayed three guitarists (Green, Spencer and Kirwan) around the rhythm section of Fleetwood and McVie. They are best represented by 1969's *Then Play On*, a milestone in progressive blues-rock. After Green's exodus in mid-1970, the remaining members recorded the lighter rock 'n' roll-oriented *Kiln House*. Early in 1971, a born-again Spencer abruptly left the band during a US tour to join the Children of God.

The second key configuration found Fleetwood, McVie and Kirwan joined by McVie's wife, Christine, on keyboards and guitarist Bob Welch, a Southern Californian who became the group's first US member and a harbinger of new directions. This configuration produced a pair of musical masterpieces, *Future Games* (1971) and *Bare Trees* (1972). Kirwan, who was having personal problems, was asked to leave in August 1972. The remaining foursome were joined by Dave Walker (vocals) and Bob Weston and recorded *Penguin* in 1973 (the bird became their band's logo) and *Mystery to Me* (1974). Weston left and the remaining members released *Heroes Are Hard to Find* that same year.

Above: McVie, Green, Kirwan, Spencer and Fleetwood – the definitive early Fleetwood Mac.

The third 'definitive' version of Fleetwood Mac came together in 1975 with the recruitment of Lindsay Buckingham and Stevie Nicks. The San Francisco duo had previously recorded together as Buckingham-Nicks. Drummer Fleetwood heard a tape of theirs and the pair were recruited without so much as a formal audition. This proved to be far and away Fleetwood Mac's most durable and successful line-up.

In addition to the most solid rhythm section in rock, the group contained strong vocalists and songwriters in Buckingham, Nicks and Christine McVie. Male and female counterpoints were offered with unusual candour on the watershed albums *Fleetwood Mac* (1975) and *Rumours* (1977). *Fleetwood Mac* introduced the revitalised group with such sparkling tracks as 'Over My Head', Fleetwood Mac's first-ever US Top 40 single; 'Rhiannon', which became Nicks' haunting signature song; 'Say You Love Me', which showed off the group's three-part harmonies; and the driving 'Monday Morning'. *Rumours* was written and recorded as three long-term relationships – between Buckingham and Nicks, the McVies, and Fleetwood and his wife – publicly unravelled. The album is an emotional document of romantic turmoil that reflects the interpersonal upheavals of the promiscuous 1970s and resonated with their audience with songs that had an enduring appeal. Among them were the US Top 10 hits 'Go Your Own Way', 'Dreams', 'Don't Stop' and 'You Make Loving Fun'. Fleetwood Mac toured for seven months and were the most popular group in the world at that time. *Rumours* has to date sold over 20 million copies. Fleetwood Mac have sold more than 70 million albums since their inception.

Under the creative direction of Lindsay Buckingham, whose skill as a producer and pop visionary became increasingly evident, Fleetwood Mac grew more

experimental with the double album *Tusk*, released in 1979. Band members then pursued their solo careers for three years, followed by another extensive tour. Stevie Nicks, in particular, nurtured a career that rivalled Fleetwood Mac's for popularity.

Fleetwood Mac released two studio albums in the Eighties – *Mirage* (1982) and *Tango in the Night* (1987) – but its front-line members were increasingly drawn to their solo careers. Disinclined to tour, Buckingham announced he was leaving shortly after *Tango in the Night* was released. He was replaced by guitarists Billy

Burnette and Rick Vito, who appeared on the 1990 album *Behind the Mask*. Eventually, both Nicks and Christine McVie revealed they, too, would no longer tour with Fleetwood Mac. Nicks officially left the band a month after Fleetwood Mac regrouped to perform 'Don't Stop' at President Bill Clinton's inauguration in January 1993. The core members, Fleetwood and McVie, recruited guitarist Dave Mason and singer Bekka Bramlett, but the link in Fleetwood Mac's chain had been broken one too many times and this line-up's one album, *Time* (1995) was not well-received.

In 1997, Fleetwood Mac's classic line-up set aside their differences for a reunion that marked the 30th anniversary of the original group's founding and the 20th anniversary of the release of *Rumours*. A concert was filmed for an MTV special and saw release on video and audio formats as *The Dance*; it found the group revisiting old material and premiering new songs. A fully-fledged reunion tour followed. The band members continue to pursue successful careers.

Above: Stevie Nicks fronting Fleetwood Mac.

20TH CENTURY BOYS – GLAM ROCK

The melting pot of 1970s rock produced many different kinds of stars. A new genre of music began to form when rock stars became more sexually ambiguous. Rock had previously always given the public guitar heroes who epitomised the American red-blooded male, half-cowboy, half-Hell's Angel, with their leather jackets and blue jeans. In the UK, art schools had often been the birthplace of our rock stars but now they were becoming the essential background for the new superstars of a generation. Not only did they dress like girls, they wore make-up like girls – this was art. The first of these fantastical rockers was called Marc Bolan.

BIOGRAPHY:

Marc Bolan

Marc Bolan was born Mark Feld and began to play guitar aged nine. After working as a mod fashion model he later performed as the folk musician Toby Tyler. Obsessed with fantasy themes, he signed with Decca in 1965, adopting the stage name Marc Bolan, under which he released a single called 'The Wizard'. Leaving Decca, the singer-songwriter worked with a group called John's Children for about a year, then, in 1967, formed the group Tyrannosaurus Rex with bongo player Steve Took (born Steve Turner).

Discovered by then-fledgling DJ John Peel, Tyrannosaurus Rex became a popular London club band and went on to record several albums for EMI with producer Tony Visconti, who would remain essential to the group's success. With UK Top 40 singles like 'Debora', Tyrannosaurus Rex's first LP, the acoustic Pink Floyd-inspired *My People Were Fair And Had Sky In Their Hair ... But Now They're Content To Wear Stars On Their Brows*, reached No 15 on the British charts, despite having one of the longest album titles in music history. After releasing 1968's *Prophets, Seers And Sages: The Angels of the Ages* Bolan, now a cult elfin figure, released a popular book of mythic poetry. In 1969 their *Unicorn* album was released, after which Took was replaced with percussionist Mickey Finn for the group's final, partly electric album, 1970's *A Beard of Stars*.

Above: Fantastical rocker Marc Bolan.

became a hallmark of glam rock, featured work from Bolan's associate David Bowie, and spawned the UK No 1 single 'Metal Guru' and the No 2 single 'Children of the Revolution'. 1973's *Tanx* was followed by the UK No 4 single 'The Groover'. Having sold 39 million albums and charted 10 UK Top 5 singles, T. Rex were beginning to wane, overshadowed by Bowie. Drummer Bill Legend left the group and was replaced by Davey Lutton for the 1974 *Zinc Alloy* album.

Bolan's Zip Gun was the group's first album recorded without producer Tony Visconti although keyboardist Dino Dines was used. In 1976 Bolan disbanded T. Rex and recorded an album, *Dandy in the Underworld*, with a set of session musicians; it was supported by a tour with the Damned – a merger between glam and punk.

In 1970 Tyrannosaurus Rex became T. Rex, with Bolan and Finn releasing a UK No 2 single called 'Ride a White Swan'. T. Rex's first electric guitar-driven album sold well and the duo was more popular than ever, appealing to teenage girls rather than older hippies. After putting glitter around his eyes and dropping the fantasy-themed lyrics in favour of teenage anthems, Bolan launched T. Rex into the future – the world's first 'glam' band. With the addition of bassist Steve Currie and drummer Bill Legend, the now-quartet recorded the single 'Hot Love', which reached No 1 in the UK. The group's next single, 'Get It On' ('Bang a Gong' in the US), reached No 1 in Britain and No 10 in the United States, setting the stage for the UK No 1 success of the their next album, *Electric Warrior*.

Now one of the most popular groups in Britain, T. Rex re-negotiated with EMI and formed their own label, allowing Bolan greater artistic control of his music. The group's next single, 'Telegram Sam', reached No 1 in Britain. 1972's *The Slider*, whose proto-metal riffs

T. Rex came to a tragic end. Bolan had just started writing songs with David Bowie when he died in a car crash on 16 September 1977. T. Rex bassist Steve Currie also died in an auto accident, four years later and percussionist Steve Took choked to death in 1980. The music they played was a bubbly brand of rock that still sounds fresh today.

While Bolan was the elfin dandy of the 20th century, his friend David Bowie is the ever-changing chameleon.

BIOGRAPHY:
David Bowie

David Jones was born in South London in 1947. He entered the music scene as a choirboy and then sang with the Manish Boys and the Lower Third in the early 1960s, before embarking on a solo career in 1966. In 1969, the year that Neil Armstrong walked on the moon, Bowie landed his first hit, the moody, existential 'Space Oddity' which reached No 5. On the strength of such early albums as *The Man Who Sold the World*, Bowie became a cult figure. He was an inspired artist and his fame came with *The Rise and Fall of Ziggy Stardust and the Spiders from Mars* (1972). The 'Spiders' included the late guitarist Mick Ronson with his proto-heavy metal guitar riffs. This album and its roadshow is considered the ultimate in glam rock.

Bowie was one of the first to blend rock with theatre by creating his provocative alter ego Ziggy Stardust. He evolved from cult figure to rock icon in Ziggy's wake. He dressed the part of the flamboyant 'starman', affecting costumes that fused British mod and Japanese kabuki styles. Rainbow-hued body suits, metallic bomber jackets, space-samurai outfits, white satin kimonos and see-through mesh tops were among the fanciful threads worn by Bowie in the guise of Ziggy Stardust and his successor, the paranoid androgynous Aladdin Sane. Bowie also displayed his affection for the mod 'London underground' of the mid-to-late 1960s with *Pin-Ups*, an album on which he covered songs by the Pretty Things, Pink Floyd, Them and other hit-makers of the day.

Through the 1970s, Bowie pioneered and embodied the notion of rock style. For much of the decade he projected a calculated aloofness, and many wondered where the characters ended and the 'real Bowie' began. However, Bowie took refuge from fame – and a drug problem – in Berlin, where he embarked on a fruitful union with producer Brian Eno that resulted in the celebrated 'Berlin trilogy': three largely experimental, atmospheric albums on which Bowie reinvented himself yet again. With *Low*, *Heroes* and *The Lodger*, Bowie peeled away his masks while creating music that anticipated the ambient and industrial soundscapes of the future.

Above: David Bowie and Mick Jagger collaborated for Live Aid.

In 1980, Bowie released *Scary Monsters*, which summed up and closed the door on the previous decade. The album even cast a final nod to Bowie's 'Major Tom' character from 'Space Oddity' with the sequel 'Ashes to Ashes'. Moving into acting, Bowie worked on Broadway for four months in 1980, receiving rave reviews for his portrayal of John Merrick in the lead role of *The Elephant Man*. Musically, Bowie's commercial masterstroke came in 1983 with *Let's Dance*, an accessible album of dance music that gave Bowie his second No 1 hit with the brassy, swaggering title track, as well as 'China Girl' and 'Modern Love'. That same year, the D.A. Pennebaker-produced film documentary of Bowie's final tour from the Ziggy days, entitled *Ziggy Stardust/The Motion Picture*, was released.

Admittedly, Bowie didn't dominate and define the 80s as he did the 1970s. However, he released intermittent albums (*Tonight* in 1984 and *Never Let Me Down* in 1987) and collaborated with Queen, Mick Jagger, Bing Crosby and the Pat Metheny Band while further pursuing his lifelong interest in alternative media, including film, theatre and painting. In 1989, the Ryko label reissued Bowie's back catalogue – from *Space Oddity* through to *Scary Monsters*, as well as singles compilations and a spectacular box set, *Sound + Vision*. Bowie supported the reissue program with the Sound + Vision Tour, during which he performed a largely retrospective repertoire for what he claimed would be the last time. He also formed a band, Tin Machine, submerging his ego as an equal member of this edgy, hard-rocking entity. *Tin Machine* did not achieve the commercial or critical acclaim of Bowie's solo work, but the very idea of Bowie as a band-mate spoke intriguingly of his more human side.

In April 1992, Bowie married the Somalian model Iman at a civil ceremony in Lausanne, Switzerland. He commemorated the event with 'The Wedding', from the 1993 album *Black Tie White Noise*. Subsequently, Bowie embarked on a startlingly ambitious and uncompromising series of albums. The unsettling *Outside* (1995) was a self-described 'non-linear Gothic Drama Hyper-cycle' based on characters from a Bowie short story. The accompanying tour found him joined by the industrial rock band Nine Inch Nails. In 1997, Bowie released *Earthling*, an album that showed the influence of the underground dance-music scene on Bowie (and vice versa). A year later, he was the first rock star to become an Internet Service Provider (ISP). The autobiographical, angst-filled *hours...* appeared in 1999, providing mortal musings from Bowie on the eve of the new millennium. He is now a cyber rock star as his latest releases are available through the internet.

While Bolan and Bowie only played with gender, Freddie Mercury broke the final taboo by being the first superstar to reveal his homosexuality to the general public. Had he done this even a decade earlier he would have been ostracised, not only by the record industry but by society in general. But the times, as Bob Dylan said, were a-changing. Freddie Mercury's band were the aptly named Queen.

Queen

Queen began in early 1971, when Brian May (guitar) and Roger Taylor (drums) from the defunct group Smile joined with local singer Freddie Mercury (born Freddie Bulsara) and college classmate John Deacon (bass). The group played small London shows before a demo found its way to EMI and they signed with them in early 1973. Their debut album *Queen* was released that July. Although it was not hugely successful it got them a break as support for Mott the Hoople. *Queen II*, their 1974 follow-up, was to be followed by a UK and US tour, but May was hospitalised and many of the US shows were cancelled.

The group's third album, *Sheer Heart Attack*, and their single 'Killer Queen', reached No 2 in the charts. After a sold-out world tour and a management change, Queen returned in late 1975 with the elaborately recorded album *A Night at the Opera*, whose advance single, 'Bohemian Rhapsody', reached No 1 despite being six minutes long. The album was a huge success, reaching the US Top 10 and going platinum.

During the world tour that followed, each of Queen's first four albums sat in the UK Top 20, an unprecedented accomplishment. They were popular in Japan as well, being mobbed by fans at each performance.

Queen played a free concert in London's Hyde Park in September 1976 in anticipation of the release of *A Day at the Races*. The album was met with record advance orders in Britain, and reached No 5 in the United States. After a US tour and a Roger Taylor solo single, the group staged an expensively elaborate European tour, part of which was filmed for a video. 1977's *News of the World*,

which brazenly flew in the face of punk rock with its overblown production, contained the international No 1 hits 'We Will Rock You' and 'We Are The Champions', utilised as sport and film anthems ever since.

In 1978 they released *Jazz*, which featured a controversial photo of an all-female nude bicycle race staged by the band in Wimbledon Stadium. After more extensive touring, Queen returned to London in 1979 to record their double live album, *Live Killers*. The group recorded the *Flash Gordon* movie soundtrack in 1980. Incorporating synthesisers into their already grandiose sound, Queen next produced 1980's *The Game*, the biggest album of their career and their first US No 1 album. Their single 'Another One Bites the Dust' reached No 1 in the US rock, disco and soul categories simultaneously. The quartet undertook the first-ever tour of South America by a major rock band, playing to crowds of unheard-of sizes – up to 130,000 people per date. In fact, the band was perhaps bigger in South America than in the rest of the world, with Queen singles staying at No 1 for years at a time.

In early 1981 Roger Taylor released his solo debut, *Fun in Space*. During the group's time off, EMI released a 'greatest hits' album which stayed in the Top 100 for years. The following year Queen released *Hot Space*, another commercial success. After pausing to release a Brian May solo EP, *Star Fleet Project*, a Japanese TV show soundtrack, Queen returned to the studios in late 1983 to record *The Works*. Released in 1984, its first single 'Radio Ga Ga', reached No 1 in 19 countries, although it was not as popular as past Queen releases.

Above: The memorable cover of Queen's second album.

Following the release of another Roger Taylor solo album (*Strange Frontier*) in early 1984, Queen began another tour, this time heading to Africa. Their decision to include South Africa, then under boycott due to its racial policies, caused the band to be heavily criticised and they even faced protests at some New Zealand concert dates. Freddy Mercury's solo debut, *Mr Bad Guy*, was released in 1985, shortly before Queen appeared at the famous Live Aid show in London that July. The group took some time off before recording a soundtrack for the 1986 action film *Highlander*, entitled *A Kind of Magic*. The complicated tour that followed included a stop in Hungary, one of the first appearances by a Western rock band in an Eastern Bloc country; the tour culminated with a massive show at Knebworth that drew 120,000 British fans. The tour was captured on the group's second live album, *Live Magic*.

Queen spent much of 1987 and 1988 apart – Taylor formed a new band, the Cross, while Mercury worked on *Barcelona*, a duet album recorded with opera star Montserrat Caballé. Queen's much-anticipated 16th album, *The Miracle*, was released in May 1989, entering the UK charts at the top. After another break to pursue solo projects, they signed a new US deal with Hollywood Records, who released the band's back catalogue on CD. 1991's *Innuendo* once again entered the UK charts at No 1, reaching the US Top 30.

On 22 November 1991, singer Freddie Mercury shocked the rock world by admitting that he was dying of AIDS. Two days later, he passed away, effectively ending Queen. Ironically, only a few months after Mercury's death, Queen enjoyed an amazing revival in the US, thanks to the appearance of 'Bohemian Rhapsody' in the movie *Wayne's World*. A massive Freddie Mercury memorial concert was staged in

London to raise money for AIDS awareness, with appearances by acts such as Elton John, Guns 'n' Roses and David Bowie. The televised concert was reportedly seen by over one billion people world-wide.

After Mercury's death, Brian May released his second solo album, *Back to the Light*, in 1993, while Roger Taylor continued performing with the Cross; Deacon briefly retired from music. The three Queen members recorded music in 1994 to accompany unreleased Mercury demo tapes, creating the final Queen album, 1995's *Made In Heaven*. As musicians they reunite every so often, most recently recording with Robbie Williams for the soundtrack to *A Knight's Tale*.

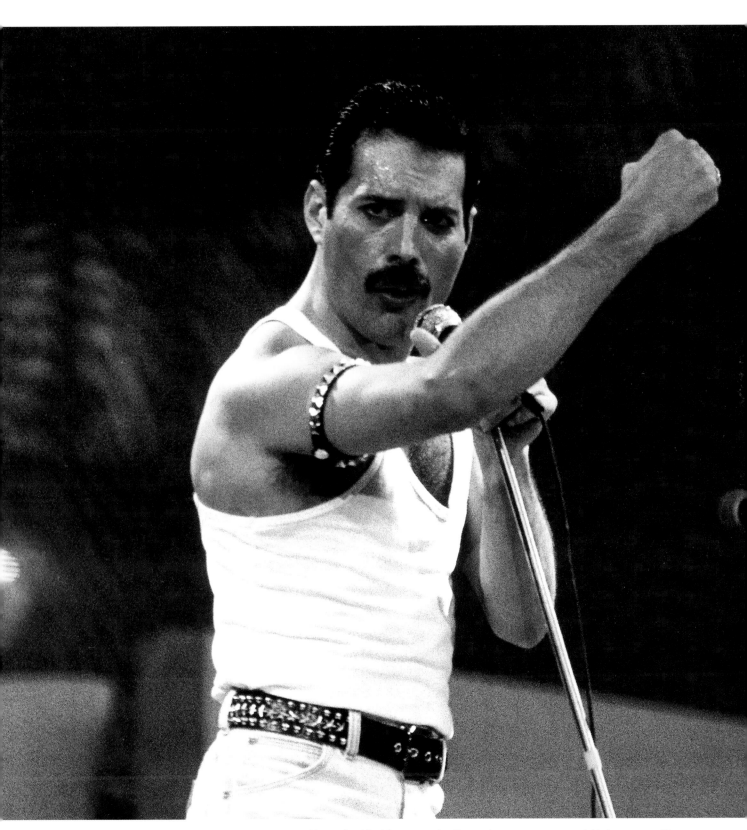

Above: Freddie Mercury – the first rock superstar to reveal his homosexuality.

PRETTY VACANT – PUNK ROCK

For every action there is a reaction and gradually a new style of rock emerged. Many musicians had had enough of the glamorous extravaganzas that were being made up by the record companies. They wanted a return to a simpler, more accessible style of rock 'n' roll, music that could be played again in smaller venues without the technical complications that stadium rock required, a music that could be played by almost anyone who aspired to it, a music that was to blow a raspberry at its own peers.

This would be called punk rock, named after the ordinary street kids, firstly of New York and then of London. Although the phenomenon became a commercial circus, it still resonates today because of that simplicity and accessibility.

The first well-known band to play in this style were from New York and were called the Ramones.

Above: The Ramones shaped the sound of New York punk rock.

BIOGRAPHY:

The Ramones

The group formed in 1974 in Forest Hills, New York, all members, although unrelated, sharing the same stage name of Ramone. The original line-up featured Joey on drums, Dee Dee sharing guitar with Johnny, and Tommy as manager. Their 20-minute sets of hard hitting but short songs earned them a recording contract before any of their contemporaries except Patti Smith. In the mid-1970s, they shaped the sound of New York punk rock with manic songs, deadpan lyrics, and an ear-bleeding wall of guitar chords.

In 1976 *Ramones* was the definitive punk album, with songs like 'Beat on the Brat', 'Blitzkrieg Bop', and 'Now I Wanna Sniff Some Glue', all 14 of them taking under 30 minutes' playing time. In 1976 the group toured England and gave the rising British punk scene the same inspiration that they gave to New Yorkers. Before the year was out, *Ramones Leave Home* had been released and they toured incessantly.

With their next two singles, the group began to soften their sound – 'Sheena is a Punk Rocker' and 'Rockaway Beach' paid their debt to 1960s styles such as bubblegum and surf music, with both reaching the lower Top 100. They were included on *Rocket to Russia*, which also contained the ballad 'Here Today, Gone Tomorrow'. At this point Tommy stopped playing with the band, preferring to function as co-producer, 'disguised' as T. Erdelyi

(his real name). His replacement was Marc Bell, henceforth dubbed Marky Ramone. His first LP with the Ramones, *Road to Ruin*, was their first to contain only 12 songs and their first to last longer than half an hour and included two singles, 'Don't Come Close' and a version of the Searchers' 'Needles and Pins'. They also had starring roles in Roger Corman's 1979 movie *Rock 'n' Roll High School*. In the early 1980s the Ramones worked with noted pop producers Phil Spector (*End of the Century*) and 10cc's Graham Gouldman (*Pleasant Dreams*), but with little commercial success. After *Subterranean Jungle*, Marky Ramone departed and was replaced by Richie Beau who became Richie Ramone. He played on four albums. One of these, *Too Tough to Die*, produced the pop single 'Howling at the Moon', recapturing some of their 70s energy, as did 'Bonzo Goes to Bitburg' off *Animal Boy*.

In 1989 the Ramones gained their widest audience by recording the title track to the soundtrack for Stephen King's *Pet Sematary*, but also underwent their greatest internal change. Dee Dee left and was replaced by C.J. Ramone. He was 14 years younger than Joey and Johnny, but the band retained their sound.

In 1994 they released *Acid Eaters*, a tribute to British 60s idols like the Animals and the Rolling Stones. With Joey sober since the start of the decade and Marky in recovery from alcoholism, they continued their relentless touring. With the release of *Adios Amigos*, the band hinted that this was their swan song. Tragically, Joey Ramone died in 2001 at the age of 49 of lymphatic cancer. Dee Dee died in 2002.

The 'Rudest Rock Band in the World' is indisputably the Sex Pistols.

BIOGRAPHY:

The Sex Pistols

Entrepreneur Malcolm McLaren put the group together during the summer of 1975. Originally called the Swankers, with lead vocalist Wally Nightingale, they soon metamorphosed into the Sex Pistols with a line-up comprising Steve Jones on guitar, Paul Cook on drums, Glen Matlock on bass and Johnny Rotten (Lydon) on vocals. By 1976 the group was playing London clubs and pubs and boasted a small following of teenagers, whose spiked hair, torn clothes and safety pins echoed the new fashion that McLaren was transforming into a commodity.

The group's gigs became synonymous with violence, reaching a peak during the 100 Club's Punk Rock Festival when a girl was blinded in a glass-smashing incident involving the group's most ardent follower, Sid Vicious. The group signed to EMI Records, despite the adverse publicity, and also released their first single, 'Anarchy In The UK'. From Rotten's sneering laugh at the opening of the song to the final seconds of feedback, it was an attention-grabbing debut. The Pistols had their infamous promotional interview on the London-based Today TV programme, which ended in a stream of four-letter abuse, resulting in front-page headlines in the next day's tabloid press.

More controversy ensued when the group's 'Anarchy' tour was decimated and the single suffered distribution problems and bans from shops, peaking at No 38 in the UK charts. Soon afterwards, the group was dropped from EMI in a blaze of publicity. In February 1977, Matlock was replaced by punk caricature and hanger-on Sid Vicious. In March the group was signed to A&M Records outside the gates of Buckingham Palace. One week later, A&M cancelled the contract, with McLaren picking up another parting cheque for £40,000. After reluctantly signing to Virgin Records, the group released 'God Save The Queen'. The single tore into the heart of British patriotism at a time when the populace was celebrating the Queen's Silver Jubilee. Despite a daytime radio ban the single rose to No 1 in the New Musical Express chart (No 2 in the 'official' charts, though some commentators detected skulduggery at play to prevent it from reaching the top spot). The Pistols suffered for their art as outraged royalists attacked them whenever they appeared on the streets. A third single, the melodic 'Pretty Vacant' (largely the work of the departed Matlock) again reached the Top 10. By the winter the group hit again with 'Holidays In The Sun' and issued their controversially-titled album Never Mind The Bollocks – Here's The Sex Pistols. The work rocketed to No 1 in the UK album charts amid partisan claims that it was a milestone in rock.

An ill-fated attempt to capture the group's story on film wasted much time and revenue, while a poorly received tour of America fractured the Pistols' already strained relationship. In early 1978, Rotten announced that he was leaving the group after a gig in San Francisco, although manager Malcolm McLaren claimed he was fired. McLaren, meanwhile, was intent on taking the group to Brazil in order that they could be filmed playing with the train robber Ronnie Biggs. Vicious, incapacitated by heroin addiction, could not make the trip, but Jones and Cook were happy to indulge in the publicity stunt. McLaren mischievously promoted Biggs as the group's new lead singer and another

Above: Johnny Rotten, the Pistols' sneering vocalist.

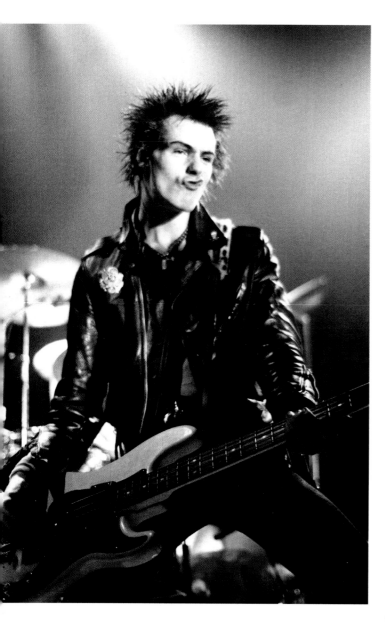

completed, the Pistols' disintegration was completed. Vicious, now the group's focal point, recorded a lame version of Eddie Cochran's 'C'mon Everybody' before returning to New York. On 12 October 1978, his girlfriend Nancy Spungen was found stabbed in his hotel room and Vicious was charged with murder. While out on bail, he suffered a fatal overdose of heroin and died in his sleep on the morning of 2 February 1979. Virgin Records continued to issue the fragments of Pistols work that they had in the can, including the appropriately titled compilation *Flogging A Dead Horse*.

The group's impact as the grand symbol of UK punk rock has ensured their longevity. The unholy saga appropriately ended in the High Court a decade later in 1986 when Rotten and his fellow ex-Pistols won substantial damages against their former manager. After years of rumour it was confirmed that the original band would re-form for one lucrative tour in 1996. The press conference to launch their rebirth was at the 100 Club in London. The usual abuse was dished out, underlining the fact that nothing had changed except the lines on their faces and rising hairlines. Their Finsbury Park debut was nostalgic rather than groundbreaking. They proved that they could still play and sweat, just like the hundreds of pretenders that have followed in their wake. Four years later Julien Temple's film documentary *The Filth And The Fury* was released to excellent reviews. It featured a mixture of archive concert footage, contemporary news reports and recent interviews with surviving members of the band.

controversial single emerged: 'Cosh The Driver'. It was later retitled 'No One Is Innocent (A Punk Prayer)' and issued as a double a-side with Vicious' disturbing rendition of the Frank Sinatra standard, 'My Way'. McLaren's movie was finally completed by director Julien Temple under the title *The Great Rock 'n' Roll Swindle*. A self-conscious rewriting of history, it callously wrote Matlock out of the script and saw the unavailable Rotten relegated to old footage. While the film was being

Paradoxically, the Sex Pistols, although giving birth to a new style of rock in the UK, also put the final nail in the coffin of the now moribund rock 'n' roll circus.

Above: Sid Vicious, the Pistols' resident punk caricature.

Since the demise of the Sex Pistols there has been an infinite number of variations on the rock 'n' roll theme. It is no longer necessary to have a guitar, musicians or even public events. All of these can and are reproduced on computers in small rooms. The new millennium's obsession with the computer has not only changed the nature of popular music but all other forms of communication.

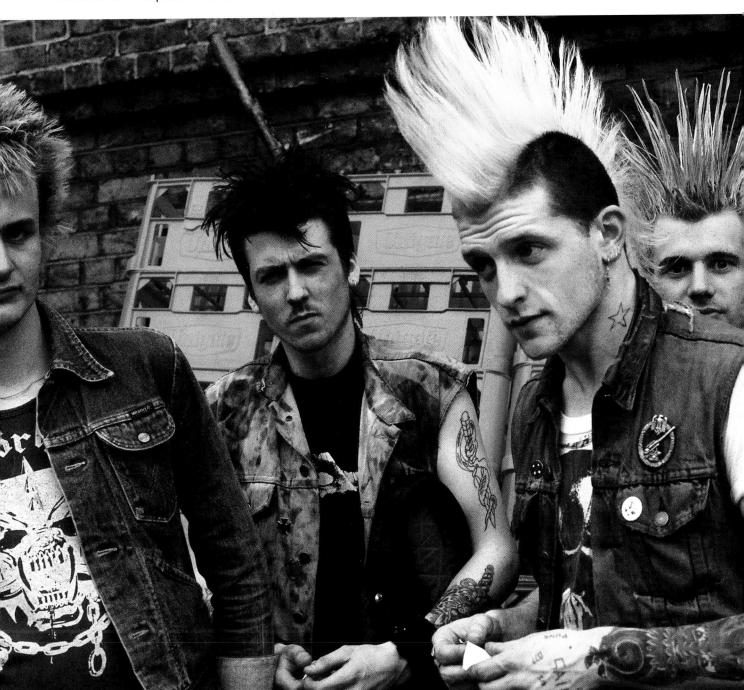

EPILOGUE

Rock 'n' roll will never die. It has always survived the changes that it has gone through over the past five decades. Somewhere a teenager is in his bedroom with a Stratocaster copy working out the same 12-bar chord sequence as the guitar heroes before him have done over the past 50 years. Like them, he dreams that one day he will be 'strutting his stuff' on stage, in front of thousands of other wannabe rock stars.

To quote Kris Kristofferson, 'I ain't saying that they beat the Devil, but they drank his beer for nothing and then they stole his songs'.

COLIN KING'S TOP 20 PLAYLIST

TITLE	ARTIST
GREAT BALLS OF FIRE	JERRY LEE LEWIS
GOOD GOLLY MISS MOLLY	LITTLE RICHARD
OH BOY	BUDDY HOLLY AND THE CRICKETS
AT THE HOP	DANNY AND THE JUNIORS
ROLL OVER BEETHOVEN	CHUCK BERRY
SUMMERTIME BLUES	EDDIE COCHRAN
HEY BO DIDDLEY	BO DIDDLEY
WOOLLY BULLY	SAM THE SHAM AND THE PHARAOHS
MONY MONY	TOMMY JAMES AND THE SHONDELLS
SHAKIN' ALL OVER	JOHNNY KIDD AND THE PIRATES
PAINT IT BLACK	THE ROLLING STONES
MY GENERATION	THE WHO
YOU REALLY GOT ME	THE KINKS
KEEP ON RUNNING	THE SPENCER DAVIS GROUP
WILD THING	THE TROGGS
BLACK DOG	LED ZEPPELIN
DANCE TO THE MUSIC	SLY AND THE FAMILY STONE
BORN TO BE WILD	STEPPENWOLF
TELEGRAM SAM	T. REX
PRETTY VACANT	THE SEX PISTOLS

INDEX